# HOW TO DATE IN A POST-DATING WORLD

# HOW
## *— to —*
# DATE

*in a*

## POST-DATING WORLD

*Diane Mapes*

SASQUATCH BOOKS
SEATTLE

Printed in Canada
Published by Sasquatch Books
Distributed by Publishers Group West
14 13 12 11 10 09 08 07 06   9 8 7 6 5 4 3 2 1

Book design: Stewart A. Williams
Author photo: ©2006 by Erik Stuhaug

Library of Congress Cataloging-in-Publication Data
Mapes, Diane.
        How to date in a post-dating world  / by Diane Mapes.
   p.  cm.
ISBN 1-57061-470-9
   1. Dating (Social customs) 2. Single people--Social life and customs--21st century. I. Title.
HQ801.M234 2006
646.7'7--dc22                                     2005057946

Sasquatch Books
119 South Main Street, Suite 400
Seattle, WA  98104
(206) 467-4300
www.sasquatchbooks.com
custserv@sasquatchbooks.com

*To my mom, who never once asked
me why I was still single*

# CONTENTS

# INTRODUCTION

D ating," according to Dr. Evelyn Millis Duvall, author of the 1958 advice book *The Art of Dating*, is "one of the most exciting periods of your life. Suddenly, there are new horizons before you. Friendships flower, your personality looms . . . This is a time of great exhilaration, splendor, and discovery. To live it fully is to enjoy one of life's most delightful experiences."

All of which raises a burning question: if dating is one of life's most delightful experiences, why is it most people these days would rather eat glass?

What's happened to the exhilaration? The splendor? The discovery? Hard to say exactly, but my guess is they were completely obliterated by the looming personality of your last Internet date. Or perhaps what you thought was a flowering friendship turned out to be chlamydia.

Let's face it, folks. Dating is no picnic these days. The bars are filled with misanthropes, the online sites with mullets, and your coupled-up friends don't help matters by setting you up with people simply because they're breathing and bipedal ("But you've got so much in common! You're both single and you're both *Homo sapiens!*"). Manners are MIA, expectations are DOA, and your love life, as a result, is totally SOL. Even if you're happy with your single status (and the popular media will be the first to tell you you're *not*), it's tough going out there. Flirting has become a foreign language, affection a damaging weakness. Instead of slowly getting to know people over drinks and dinner, we conduct brutal husband and wife interviews, impatient to hear the right answers, dismissive of all the wrong. How do you feel about children? What kind of car do you drive? Would you ever consider breast augmentations? Are those hair plugs or what? We've become shallow, we've become cranky, and we've systematically "Elimidated" true love from our lives before it can even raise its sheepish head.

Half of us are on some kind of crazed quest for the perfect soul mate, a phantom figure complete with 1,001 useful qualities ("He slices, he dices, he puts up shelves and rubs your shoulders! He's the Soul Mate 2006, now with improved communication skills!"). Others seek respite in a handful of lovers, perpetually juggling three or four at a time like colorful beanbags named Sue or Steve or Sweetie Pie. And as luck would have it, we're all swimming around in the exact same dating pool together—with no damn lifeguards to make sure we all play nice, which I suppose is where this book comes in.

Am I a dating expert? Not by a long shot (I could wax poetic on all the horrific dating mistakes I've made over the years, but I'll spare you the gory details and just ask you to trust me on this). What I am instead is incredibly curious and about as nosy as they come. So when I was asked to do this book, I went looking to the experts for answers to that age-old question: How do we date, particularly in this "post-dating" world?

I turned to the people out there in the trenches, gleaning stories and advice from nearly two hundred singles, men and women, gay and straight, young and old, heartbroken and hopeful. Then I sought out the pros, picking the brains of two dozen specialists, from social historians to sexologists, dating coaches to fashion consultants, psychologists to speed-dating entrepreneurs, experts on everything from social etiquette to serial killers to style. And finally, just for good measure, I scoured the Internet dating sites, pored over scientific research, poked around singles events, read the most recent news reports, and hit the bookshelves in order to examine a hundred years' worth of good, bad, and ugly dating advice, from *The Spinster Book* (1901) to *The Hookup Handbook* (2005).

I listened to the horror stories (really, your date threw up on you?), I asked the tough questions (why exactly is it again that men are supposed to pay for *everything*?), and I lugged home enough singles self-help to convince every bookstore clerk in Seattle that I'm pathologically obsessed with finding a man.

The end result, you hold in your hands a grab bag of observations, advice, and historical tidbits on everything from good grooming to bungled breakups, social networks to naked speed dating.

How do we date in a world where a hundred years of conflicting customs, shifting social mores, and a consumer-crazed society have made it easier to get our own reality TV show than find someone we actually like? The same way we learn to swim--by taking a deep breath and diving in.

# PART ONE

# ARE YOU READY TO DATE?

*The world of dating is a wonderful world—for most people.*

—ART UNGER, EDITOR,
*DATEBOOK'S COMPLETE GUIDE TO DATING*, 1960

# WHAT IS DATING?

*Dates afford a person the opportunity to study the conduct and behavior, the attitude and capabilities, of a number of people, and finally make an intelligent choice in selecting a partner who conforms most to his "ideal." Dating, therefore, should not be discouraged.*

—ALFRED L. MURRAY,
YOUTH'S COURTSHIP PROBLEMS, 1940

Dating means different things to different people. To Darryl, a 28-year-old project manager from Seattle, it's a way to "find the right person with whom I'm completely compatible and willing to commit my life." For Kate, a 26-year-old single from San Francisco, it's when "two people go out and the man pays."

It's a little more complicated for Eric, a 27-year-old teacher from Iowa City. "A date is a nebulous thing," he says. "A date could be defined by the willingness of both members of the date to label the date a date. It could be a reconnaissance date, which is simply a matter of checking out whether this person is actually going to *be* a date, in which case the date is merely a preemptory event toward an actual date: It's a neo-date. There's also the school of thought that says any scheduled appointment in which the situation is casual and not business-related is a date. I tend to go with the more direct belief that a date is a date if and only if it is labeled a date by one or both members of the date. Otherwise, it's simply dinner or drinks with a friend."

No wonder we're all having problems—we can't even come up with a simple definition without tying ourselves into some kind of Gordian word knot.

It gets even crazier when you consider the number of people who refuse to label dates as dates. They don't date, they "hang out" or "hook up." To these people, dating seems to imply the presence of corsages, convertibles, and possibly even the scariest C-word of all, commitment, even if you're simply committing to the fact that you're *on* a date. "I do my best to avoid dating," writes Greg, a fortysomething bookseller from Seattle. "I prefer hanging out and getting to know women that way. I'm probably just engaging in semantics or deluding myself."

Could be, Greg, but you're certainly not alone.

Like a career criminal, dating has gone by a number of different aliases over the years—spooning, sparking, courting, calling, bundling, fussing, stepping out, pitching woo, getting it on, kicking it. And the code of conduct governing this odd and lovely ritual has been equally malleable. But no matter what you call it and no matter how you define it, most people would probably agree that dating is the process we all have to go through in order to get intimate with someone—in either a romantic or a sexual sense.

"Dating? I guess I'd define dating as the four hours of foreplay before I have sex," says Wendell, a massage therapist from Seattle.

Some people prefer their dates to have the life span of a mayfly. Others are in it for the long haul—dating is just the first leg of that long journey to marital bliss. But whether you're looking for a Friday night hookup or a fabulous new husband, it's nice to know that the person you're looking at is prepared. And from all accounts, many are not.

Some are shell-shocked from divorce, others seething with anger over a recent—or not so recent—relationship misdeed. Still others reek of desperation or Drakkar Noir, or they just plain reek. Their manners are awful, their humor nonexistent; they say they're looking for long-term companionship but all they really want is a short-term sexual poultice. Simply put, they're just not ready to be out there.

# Common Post-Dating Acronyms

**ADULT:** Code word for explicit sexual content, as in "adult site"

**BBW, BHM:** Big beautiful woman, big handsome man

**BDSM:** Bondage and discipline, domination and submission, sado-masochism

**420:** Pot-friendly

**FWB:** Friends with benefits

**GWM:** Gay white male

**HPV:** Human papilloma virus

**HWP:** Height/weight proportionate, i.e., "normal" size (whatever that is)

**ISO:** In search of

**MWM:** Married white male

**NSA:** No strings attached, as in "NSA sex"

**PANSEXUAL:** Not the act of having sex with pans, but rather being open to a variety of sexual activities

**PDA:** Public display of affection

**PLAY:** Often a code word for someone interested in exploring an open relationship or even BDSM

**SAF:** Single Asian female

**STD:** Sexually transmitted disease

**TOP, BOTTOM, VERS:** Roles in BDSM or positions in gay sex ("vers" means versatile)

# CHAPTER 1

# LET'S TALK ABOUT HYGIENE AND GROOMING

*It is doubtful if there is anything more destructive to romance than soiled underwear or body odor.*
—ERNEST BURGESS AND MORRIS FISHBEIN,
*SUCCESSFUL MARRIAGE*, 1947

I t seems obvious, but some people have a tendency to forget the little things in life that can mean so much to those around them, like, um, bathing. Once you're coupled up and complacent, you might be able to get away with a skipped shower or that thatch of greasy hair, but if you're planning on entering the high-stress world of competitive dating, you'd better learn fast that people will absolutely *not* love you for you. Especially if you smell a bit like old socks.

According to the *Standard Textbook of Cosmetology* (circa 1938), the seven basic requirements for good personal hygiene include cleanliness, posture, exercise, relaxation, adequate sleep, balanced diet, and (my personal favorite) wholesome thoughts. While most of us do our best to exercise, eat right, stand up straight, and sleep, it would appear that some of us could use a little improvement when it comes to one particular category.

## WASH YOUR BODY

In a 2005 survey of twenty-seven thousand people conducted by MSNBC.com and *Elle* magazine, both men and women indicated that the absolute number-one turnoff of all time was bad body odor.

> FUN FACT: According to a recent survey by the Emily Post Institute, the number-two "fashion emergency" encountered at work involves a co-worker with either serious body odor or excessive perfume/aftershave.

In other words, people really hate it when you stink; in fact, it appears to be the best way *not* to get a date.

"Stinky dates are always a deal breaker," says Carly, a 40-year-old from Jersey City. "What's up with men who can't smell themselves? Or people who are *always* a smelly mess?"

What's up with that indeed? In today's product-heavy world (where you can practically find free bars of soap in your cereal box), there's really no reason for anyone to go around smelling bad. Or is there?

If you're doing your daily ablutions and find you're still a little off, you could be experiencing a drug reaction. Or infection. Check in with your doctor to see if there's something weird going on. Otherwise, follow the guidelines provided by the *Standard Textbook of Cosmetology* (and your mother) and "keep the body fresh and dainty by having a daily shower or bath and by using an underarm deodorant."

Maybe you do shower every morning, like clockwork. But then you scurry through an urban obstacle course, sweat through a bunch of high-powered meetings, and do an hour of hot yoga after work. It's no surprise that by 7 p.m., you're a tad ripe. As that sweet young thing sitting next to you at the bar is about to find out.

If you have a date—or if you think you might possibly run into someone you might *like* to date—do yourself (and their nose) a favor and get yourself cleaned up, and not just with a spit bath and a few splashes of Eternity. Use soap, water, a clean towel, a dash of powder or perfume (not too much!). Remember, love doesn't *have* to stink.

## FIX YOUR HAIR

According to Sophie C. Hadida, author of *Manners for Millions* (1950), "no one but a sloven would neglect the daily arrangement of the hair." And yet, unwashed hair or a bad haircut ranked high on the list of top turnoffs for men and women in the *Elle*/MSNBC. com survey.

People like clean hair. It's pretty, it smells good, and it doesn't make you gag when it gets caught in your mouth while you're making out.

So wash your hair, folks. Maybe not every day. Maybe not every other day. But at least more than this guy:

"When I was in high school, I dated a guy who lived about an hour away from me," says Molly, a 27-year-old single from Minneapolis. "I saw him maybe once a month, and one day he came over to my house and had a revelation. 'What a coincidence,' he said. 'I washed my hair today, and the last time I washed my hair was the last time I saw you!' It had been at least five weeks since I'd seen him!"

## WATCH YOUR MOUTH

As it turns out, bad breath is right behind body odor as another top turnoff, with crooked and discolored teeth nipping at its heels.

It would appear we need to watch our mouths.

What's the best way to achieve clean, fresh breath? By practicing good oral hygiene. According to the American Dental Association, that means (1) brush your teeth twice a day, (2) floss daily, (3) eat a balanced diet and cut back on the snickersnacks (please note: snickersnacks is not an official ADA phrase), and (4) go in for check-ups on a regular basis.

What if your breath still smells like old potatoes? In the short term, you might want to invest in some strong breath mints or a few of those little pocket pack thingies. But for the long term, try to figure out what's causing the problem. In addition to the steps above, try brushing your tongue. If that doesn't take care of the problem, then see your dentist or even your doctor for additional help. (Of course, if nothing helps, you can always keep your mouth shut and, instead of foul breath, exude an aura of mystery.)

But fresh breath is just part of that all-important oral equation. Your choppers count for a lot as well. In fact, according to the beauty guide *Mirror, Mirror on the Wall* (1960), "your teeth can make or destroy your beauty," as Andrew, a 46-year-old single from Chicago, can attest.

### Say Cheese!

*I'd been in correspondence with this woman via the Internet and made arrangements to meet her at a bookstore/coffee shop early on a weekend afternoon. I arrived at the appointed time, looked around and saw, from behind, a petite blonde. She turned, our eyes met, she smiled—and she had no front teeth. None! My advice to young ladies entering the dating pool: even before you buy that new computer, invest in some teeth.*

Of course, many people *are* investing in their teeth—whitening them, straightening them, or yanking the damn things out and starting afresh with a brand-new set. Invisible braces, bleaching strips, dental implants—there's no end to the things we can put in our mouths.

If you feel it's warranted, by all means take advantage of the latest oral wonders. But don't forget to utilize one of the most low-tech dating secrets of all time, and simply learn to smile.

## CLEAN YOUR HOUSE

There's something to be said for style. And there's something else entirely to be said for squalor: it's pretty gross. If you're thinking about entering the dating scene, make sure your house is in order—in both a metaphorical and a literal sense.

Wearing clothes from the bottom of the laundry hamper is not acceptable, no matter how much you'd like to persuade yourself that wrinkling and stains are part of the natural beauty of the fabric. Nor is skipping off to meet someone with food encrusted on your clothes.

"I went on one of those pre-dates with a guy I met on Match. com," says Renate, a 33-year-old single from Santa Fe. "And the guy shows up in a gray sweat suit, with dried food dribbled all the way down the front of his shirt."

Show respect to yourself and the people you're interacting with by wearing clean, presentable clothes. And that goes double if you're going dancing.

"I can take the smell of sweat, but the smell of old sweat is just foul," said Debra, a 47-year-old single from Seattle. "I don't know what it is about polypropylene, but it really stinks if you don't wash it. Whenever I go out dancing, there's always some polypro guy who hasn't learned yet that you *have* to wash your clothes."

And the same goes for your car. If you're going to be sharing your vehicle with anyone—particularly a potential lover—take a moment to clean out all the beer cans, the hamburger wrappers, and the dirty laundry before you leave home.

"I went on a blind date with this woman who said she had two dogs," says Rob, 37, of Seattle. "Which I guessed by the quarter inch of dog hair layering the carpet of her car. It looked like she had never vacuumed it out—ever. We never went out again."

Obviously, a clean home is also crucial, particularly if you have an inkling that a date might go well. If your dirty dishes have more fur than your cat or your laundry pile is bigger than your bed, either clean up or avoid inviting anyone back to your place. Unless they're a maid.

It's a jungle out there, folks, a hotbed of cutthroat competition. Like it or not, people are jaded and cynical and looking to reject you as quickly and effortlessly as they possibly can. One false step and you'll be voted off the dating island—it's as simple as that. So don't give them any extra ammunition. Wash your body, take out your trash, do your laundry, and floss every day. It's a great first step toward getting yourself ready to meet your match. But it's not the only one you'll need to take.

## GOOD GROOMING IS IMPORTANT, TOO

*It's good manners to look your best 99 percent of the time, because you make most people around you feel comfortable when you take the trouble to keep yourself shipshape . . . When you look crummy, it's awfully easy to act that way. Especially on a date.*

—SANDI CUSHMAN,
*HANDBOOK OF DATING AND OTHER ETIQUETTE, 1970*

In bygone days, good grooming involved a lot of small stiff brushes and weird clippers, wooden shoe trees, and an unwieldy ironing board. These days, good grooming can involve anything from a lint roller to liposuction. A huge array of options is open to the single who wants to look their "extreme" best: personal trainers, rhinoplasty, tanning beds, breast enlargements. But it's hardly necessary to turn yourself into a plastic action figure just because you can. It is advisable, though—especially for those who have been out of the dating loop for a few months or a few years—to figure out how to be the best *you* you can be.

## YOUR SHAPE

Eating right and exercising are not only a great way to get in shape, they're both essential for your overall health and well-being. But brussels sprouts are good for us too, and nobody likes those little bastards either.

Here's the rub. If you're heading out into the dating world, you need to be aware of one crucial fact: looks are key. According to a study done by a trio of economists (two at the University of Chicago and one at MIT), looks were *the* most important variable for both men and women, at least when it came to Internet dating.

"Looks do count," says Suzanne Schlosberg, author of *The Curse of the Singles Table: A True Story of 1001 Nights Without Sex* (2004). "It's unrealistic to think otherwise. But not everybody is looking for the same thing."

Thankfully, one person's perfect body type *is* going to be vastly different from another's, and a simple Web surf will turn up all

# DICTIONARY OF DATING

## PRE-DATING TERMS

**COURTLY LOVE:** A highly romanticized kind of love, enjoyed on the sly by knights and married noblewomen during the Middle Ages and the Renaissance. Usually involved lots of longing and not so much loving.

**COURTING:** The system by which an unmarried man wooed and won (i.e., married) the woman of his dreams. Traditionally involved the exchange of flowers, small gifts, and declarations of love, either spoken or implied (through acts of violence or fainting spells).

**CALLING:** A late-nineteenth-century system of courtship in which an eligible man "called" on an eligible woman, at the invitation of either the woman or her mother. Usually involved a parlor, a piano, a bit of poetry, and a complete and utter lack of privacy. Should privacy be found, said couple might indulge in a bit of spooning, sparking, canoodling, or pitching of woo.

## DATING TERMS

**DATING:** A system of twentieth-century courtship in which couples would "go out" (usually to some paid public amusement) as opposed to staying in. This new system immediately shifted the power from women to men—or, more precisely, to men's money. Oddly enough, even when women began to earn their own keep, tradition still dictated that men ask women out, pay for the dates, and hold all the power in the relationship—except, of course, when it came to sex.

**NECKING AND PETTING:** Kissing, embracing, and caressing above the neck is known as necking. Kissing, embracing, and caressing everywhere else is known as petting. Now known as making out and foreplay, necking and petting were the scourge of the 1950s. Dating literature of the era, in fact, claimed that petting in particular could lead directly to mental illness, marital discord, and chronic congestion of the prostate.

**GOING STEADY:** Dating someone exclusively. In the 1950s, going steady was heavily discouraged because teens were the only ones doing it, primarily so they'd have a steady partner to neck and pet with. These days, everyone is in the dating pool, and going steady has transformed itself into the "committed relationship" or LTR (something we often do primarily so we'll have a steady partner to neck and pet with).

## POST-DATING TERMS

**HANGING OUT:** Keeping company with, appearing in public with, almost but not quite dating. Often employed by those who prefer to remain commitment-free.

**HOOKING UP:** Becoming romantically or sexually involved with someone. Also, marrying. Also, meeting or associating with. One of the most nebulous of the dating terms, "hooking up" covers everything from meeting somebody for a drink to having madcap sex on top of your car.

**FRIENDS WITH BENEFITS, FUCK BUDDIES:** Casual sex partners with whom you may or may not become emotionally involved.

kinds of preferences—Passionate Petite Asian Female ISO Fit Caucasian; Skinny White Guy Seeks BBW. The essential thing is to be honest about your particular type.

> **FUN FACT:** In a study on Internet dating, researchers found that only 1 percent of online daters admitted to having "less than average" looks.

"It's very important for people not to exaggerate when it comes to their looks," says Schlosberg. "On Match.com, you have to fill in a blank as to whether you're average, fit, athletic, or you have a few extra pounds. And it's pretty annoying when people exaggerate and say they're 'very fit' when clearly they're not. It's okay if you're not athletic; not everybody is looking for somebody who's very fit. But somebody who *is* looking for that is going to be mad. So it's better to be honest."

But even if we are honest about our attributes, we're still going to be judged—and sometimes judged harshly. Take it from one who knows; you may have a great smile, a loving heart, and an extremely generous nature, but it's the big butt they'll notice every time. Naturally, some folks love a big butt (god bless 'em, every one), but others can be extremely critical of a little extra junk in the trunk. Who are these people? They're called men. Like John, a 51-year-old single from Seattle.

### Who Ate My Date?

*I met this woman from out of state via the Internet and after some correspondence sent her a ticket to come and visit me (I lived in Washington, she lived in Texas). I went to the airport to pick her up and waited and waited while everyone got off the plane. And she wasn't there. Suddenly, I recognized the face of the woman I'd seen in all these photos, only it was in the middle of the face of this other person coming toward me. It sort of looked like this woman had eaten the person I was waiting for.*

*It was like that Austin Powers movie where Mike Myers plays*
*this huge fat guy and at the center of that guy's face, you can see*
*Mike Myers's little face. I wanted to just turn and walk away,*
*but I couldn't. If I'd known she was that heavy, I would not have*
*sent her a ticket. I'm just not attracted to heavy people.*

John is not alone. In the survey conducted by MSNBC.com
and *Elle* magazine, more than 31 percent of the men said they
had dumped a partner who was overweight (compared to only 12
percent of the women).

"Eighty percent of men have a thing about thin women," says
Mason Grigsby, co-author of *Love at Second Sight* (2004), a dating guide for midlife singles. "If you're an interesting woman,
you'll think the guy will want you no matter what your physical
appearance, but that's wrong. Women have to be visually appealing to men. Even men who are monstrously overweight think
women need to be perfect."

**FUN FACT:** In a study on Internet dating, researchers found that
women who posted a photo received twice as many email messages
as women who didn't. The same study found that men who reported
incomes in excess of $250,000 received 156 percent more email
messages than those with incomes of $50,000.

To be fair, it's not just the guys who care about the physical stuff. Women can be just as judgmental as their male
counterparts.

"I don't like short men," says Jenny, a 24-year-old marketer
from New York. "Or wimps. I like someone who's tall, dark, and
nice looking."

Let's face it, we're all equally shallow and despicable—every
last one of us. And even when we ourselves have flaws, we expect
perfection in others, as Jane, a 41-year-old single from Chicago,
found out.

### Mr. Knot Right

*I started corresponding with this man through Nerve.com and we decided to go to dinner. On the night of the date, he picks me up and I notice he's got a knot the size of a walnut on the right side of his bald head. WTF?! I decide to not say anything, but just wait until he mentions it. We go to the restaurant, have a nice Thai dinner and overall, I feel as if I'm doing a really good job of not staring at The Head Knot, even though I'm incredibly curious. What is it? Why does he have it? After a while, I start to feel like I'm in a David Lynch movie; I swear I even saw the thing move. We finish dinner, he heads back to my place, and I realize I'm about to get the brush-off. And I'm relieved. He's still made no mention of the knot! When he pulls up in front of my apartment, I thank him for the evening and he does the same. Then he gets this really compassionate look on his face and says, "You seem like a really nice woman, but you're just a bit too heavy for my preference. I hope you understand that I won't be calling you again." It took all my strength not to scream at him, "You've got a small alien on the side of your head but I'm too chunky?" Instead, I just said good night. He was obviously knot the man for me.*

The bottom line? Even the most pleasant among us can be exceedingly harsh when it comes to judging those we don't know, particularly if we think we might have to get naked with them. It's not that we're inherently evil; it's just that we're the product of decades of unrelenting social programming. Remember, we live in a country where *US Weekly* promoted Who's Hot Under 100 Pounds! three days before the launch of National Eating Disorders Awareness Week. Where even *opera* singers are fired for being too fat.

Embracing the increasingly vapid nature of our culture is hardly the way to go—the last thing we need is a society full of Paris Hiltons (that's *so* not hot)—but acknowledging it is key.

If you're not having any luck on the dating front, try taking a good long look in the mirror. Think about who you are and who you're trying to attract. Does your shape whisper "come hither" to someone who only hears "where's the sour cream and onion potato chips"? If so, then you've got a problem on your hands. Granted, it may be *their* problem. But you need to decide if you want to address it.

If you're comfortable with yourself just as you are, you'll no doubt find someone else who will be too—it may just take a little longer. But if you want to do something about upgrading your dating shape, there are lots of options.

"Join a gym," advises David Wygant, author of *Always Talk to Strangers* (2005). "If you can afford it, get a personal trainer. Do whatever it takes to motivate yourself. Hate the idea of a gym and envision yourself running on the treadmill like a rat on a wheel? There's a solution: Get out there and start finding alternative ways to get some exercise. Buy a bicycle. Do yoga. Walk. Run. Bowl. Do something. Work those muscles now, while you're still young enough to do it."

Trouble of it is, diet and exercise, cosmetic surgery and gastroplasty, hell, even necromancy, all take time. So how do you improve your shape quickly?

Behold the miracle of clothing.

## YOUR CLOTHES

*Looking good is not about being "fashionable" . . . It's about feeling confident.*

—CARSON KRESSLEY,

*OFF THE CUFF: THE ESSENTIAL STYLE GUIDE FOR MEN AND THE WOMEN WHO LOVE THEM*, 2004

There was a time when clothes were simply meant to keep you warm. Or keep you from running around with both your London and your France hanging out. Now, they make you. Sometimes they make you look good; other times, they make you look like a fool.

And apparently, if you know what you're doing, oftentimes they can make you look like a whole different person.

"Don't believe that the only way you can feel better about yourself is by losing weight or cosmetic surgery," TV fashionistas Trinny Woodall and Susannah Constantine write in their book *What You Wear Can Change Your Life* (2004). "You can change how you look today by learning how to show off your best assets and disguise the ones you don't like."

In other words, there's an actual science to figuring out how to dress that goes way beyond that old saw about horizontal stripes.

If you have a big ass, don't wear pants with big puffy pleats in the front and gigantic pockets on the side. If you have a fleshy back, don't cinch yourself into a bad bra that creates rolls of back flab. Whatever your unique body issue is—skinny legs, jelly belly, head knot—figure out how to wear clothes that make you look well proportioned, balanced, and put together.

Don't know how to do this? Don't worry. There are thousands of books, TV shows, personal shoppers, and gay men out there ready and willing to show you how to find clothes that not only fit properly, but are flattering for your particular body type. Tune into TLC's *What Not to Wear* with Stacy and Clinton. Watch a few episodes of *Queer Eye for the Straight Guy*. Take advantage of their knowledge and expertise. As the author of *How to Get Along with Girls* puts it, "you must employ every optical illusion of line and color to create a calculated impression." And then use a lint brush. And wear good shoes.

Even a sympathetic friend can make a world of difference to a fashion victim.

"This guy I sort of knew kept showing up to singles events wearing sneakers and sweatpants," says Lisa, a 34-year-old development director from San Francisco. "I finally went up to him and said, 'May I give you a piece of advice? Don't come to a bar looking like you're going to a gym.' He said that was how he felt most comfortable, so I told him, 'Hey, I'm comfortable in pajamas, but I certainly wouldn't go out to a bar wearing them.' Then he asked if I'd go shopping with him, and so I did. I helped him get some khakis and a button-down shirt. And after that, he started getting dates."

Guys are particularly prone to what San Francisco fashion stylist Susan Levitt calls the "hacky-sack look."

"I have a lot of very rich clients who are in the computer industry and they're still wearing khaki shorts, logo T-shirts, and baseball hats," she says. "And they look like schlumps."

What does she advise?

"Guys don't have to do the three-piece pinstriped suit with the ascot," she says. "But they shouldn't be slobs. I take my clients to Ralph Lauren, where they can get a new pair of khaki trousers, some new button-down shirts, a couple of bulky sweaters, and they look great. Guys are always so proud of some ratty shirt that they've had since college, but when you're thinking about dating, that look just doesn't cut it."

Women can be just as sloppy as men, but according to Seattle fashion consultant Rebecca Luke, they often fall victim to another problem—something she calls *Sex and the City* syndrome. "Those tight looks work fine on TV or a music video, but they don't translate well in person," she says. *"Sex and the City* is fun to watch, but to actually dress like that isn't always appropriate. It doesn't look that good and relays a different message."

What kind of message do you *not* want to relay? Ask Jeff, a 46-year-old photographer from Seattle.

### A Date with Peekaboo Patty

*I was meeting this woman once—the plan was to go out to dinner—and she shows up at the restaurant wearing some kind of tight black leather outfit that had all these holes cut in it, each hole showing off some different part of her body. She walked in and every guy in the restaurant turned to check her out. Every single guy. It was embarrassing. Plus she'd been tanning and her skin was almost orange. She looked like a gigantic carrot, for God's sake. I just thought, forget it.*

"When you're young, it's okay to go with the Britney Spears 'kinder-slut' look," says San Francisco's Susan Levitt. "The low-rise jeans, the belly-showing top, the big makeup, the hair. But once you hit age 29, you have to start dressing more age appropriate. You can still be sexy, but you need to be more of a class act."

How do you successfully navigate that thin line between sexy and slutty?

"The slutty look often happens when women don't know which part of the body to emphasize, so they emphasize all of it," says Levitt. "Just pick one or two parts to emphasize; don't do it all at the same time."

Camouflage, comfort, fit, and faux pas are just part of it. There's also that whole fashion thing. According to Carson Kressley, style sage for *Queer Eye for the Straight Guy*, clothes have an expiration date (much like food or medicine or stories about your old high school conquests). Cull old clothes—particularly those with dated looks (calling Members Only!)—out of your closet and bring in classic pieces.

Can't afford the big designer names? Don't fret—it's the look, not the label.

"You might be surprised to hear this coming from me, but it's not that important that your clothes bear a designer label," writes Kressley in *Off the Cuff*. "What's most important is the look, fit, and quality."

If you're on a budget, Kressley suggests you look for designer duds and classic pieces at discount chains like T. J. Maxx, Marshall's, or Filene's or at consignment shops or even upscale vintage-clothing stores. In the meantime, save your pennies so you can buy the real deal down the line. Just as with people, quality lasts.

## FINISHING TOUCHES

*An ugly nose can be made less prominent with the proper make-up and hat.*

—W. S. KEATING,
*HOW TO GET ALONG WITH BOYS*, 1945

Of course, there's more to preparing for the exciting world of dating than just making sure you have a fit body and a fun wardrobe.

Get a haircut that's current—you might even consider highlights to bring out the green in your eyes. Instead of inviting ridicule with a comb-over, exude confidence with your hair proudly cropped short or shaved clean off (trust me, a smooth, bald head is très touchable). If facial hair is your thing, make sure it's trimmed and neat and completely free of cheese crumbles.

Worried about your nails? Then spring for a manicure and/or pedicure. Glasses the only thing dating you with any regularity? Then buy some new frames.

Guys, get some clippers and take care of those wild hairs protruding from your ears, your nose, or wherever else they might be lurking. Girls, would it kill you to try a new lipstick? And if you tend to put your paint on with a trowel, then perhaps what you really need is a make*under*.

"Makeup is a lot like clothing," says Susan Levitt. "You have to choose what you want to emphasize, either your eyes or your lips. You can't do both up, or you're going to look like a clown. It's also important to note that as you age, you have to change your look, lighten it up, and focus on your best part. You can't just pack on the spackle."

What if you don't know the difference between complex collagen and a high colonic? Then take a number and stand in line.

"There are a lot of gals lost in the makeup world," says Levitt. "But you really do need to learn how to apply makeup, to find out what works for your complexion. If you don't know how to do your makeup, I recommend going to some gay guy who's been at the Chanel counter for ten years and have him help you out. Go for quality, not quantity. Fewer pieces, but better pieces."

Ah, and then there's that mysterious fifth sense—smell. According to *Always Ask a Man: Arlene Dahl's Key to Femininity* (1965), "Perfume, used with discretion, can be a powerful, invisible ally." Please note her use of the word *discretion*, something that was missing in New Yorker Neal's dating experience.

### *Really Bad Scent of a Woman*

*Way back when, I went with a friend and two lovely girls to some Ingmar Bergman films. It was a double feature—both of them dense and horrible and tortured—but the real torture was off-screen. One of the girls was wearing a horrid-smelling scent. I will never forget that experience or that nasty smell. Four hours in a movie theater watching impossible films with that smell all around me. I was completely repelled.*

Naturally, there are those who will feel that all of this rigmarole for the sake of finding somebody to make out with is utter nonsense. These people balk at the thought of wearing the tiniest speck of makeup or shaving that five o'clock shadow or going out on the town in anything other than their favorite mud-encrusted Reeboks. Anything else is subterfuge, they argue. It's deceitful, dishonest: It's not *real*. Would these people show up for a job interview in their bathrobe and bunny slippers? Of course not; they know how important a good first impression is in the business world. Well, the dating world is no different.

"A good friend of mine was corresponding with a man on the Internet," says Bonnie from Philadelphia. "And when she finally went out with him for the first time, she refused to do anything to look nice for the date. I tried to convince her to dress up or even put on a little lipstick, but she just kept saying, 'What you see is what you get.' And of course, the guy never called her back."

Shaving, wearing lipstick, or donning a nice sport coat is hardly the equivalent of selling your soul. It's just good manners. But fixating on every single feature and how you'd like to improve it—fuller lips, thinner thighs, perfectly symmetrical nose holes—is hardly necessary either.

The secret, as with all things, is balance. If you don't like the color of your teeth, by all means have them bleached. If the hair on your back is the bane of your existence, then don't walk, run to the aesthetician. Hate that mole? Burn it off. Mono-brow? Pluck away! Lose weight, gain weight, dye your hair, revamp your wardrobe. Do what you have to do to feel good about yourself, to become the best *you* you can be. But don't go nuts. Remember that with every stroke of the waxing wand or the surgeon's scalpel, you are losing a tiny piece of your individuality. Good grooming is not about becoming someone else—Duluth's answer to Britney or Whitney or Justin or George. It's about becoming your best you.

So lose the dandruff, paint the toenails, get rid of the comb-over, hell, even spring for the tummy tuck, if you feel you absolutely must. But don't go crazy and end up sacrificing your soul in the hunt for your soul mate. Keep a wart or two around just to remind yourself of who you are—and maybe to give the grand-kids something to tease you about later in life.

After all, loving yourself—flaws and all—is an important part of being ready to date.

# CHAPTER 2

# YOU AND YOUR PERSONALITY

*Personality is all the things that make you an individual, instead of one of the mob scene. It's the way you look, talk, and act . . . Not what you were born with, but what you make of yourself . . . No one is born with a friendly manner, a pleasant speaking voice, or conversational ability! All of these things are developed, along with character and your general outlook on life.*

—GAY HEAD,
BOY DATES GIRL, 1949

We've all gone out with people who are obviously not emotionally ready to climb onto the dating-go-round and yet they're still out there, circling away. Maybe their self-confidence has taken a sabbatical, or they're exceedingly bitter or heartbroken over a bad breakup. Or maybe they're just plain, you know, nuts. How do you know when you or somebody you may be going out with is emotionally well groomed? A quick consult with a certified therapist is probably the best way. But there are a few things even an ordinary single can figure out.

# THE WALKING WOUNDED

*Getting over a broken heart is a hard and lonely business.*

—Dr. Evelyn Millis Duvall,
*The Art of Dating*, 1958

The heartbreak hotel is a horrible place to wind up. Your chest is full of wet sawdust, your contacts are caked with salt. Life lacks color, poetry, significance. Why? Because you foolishly made some sketchy plans for a seemingly happy future, and now those plans, along with your pride and self-confidence (and possibly even your bank account), have been thoroughly decimated.

Where can you go? What do you do? You try the online dating sites, but all you find are pictures of people with the same brown eyes as your ex. You go out on the town with your buds and spend the evening feigning interest in one person's miniature golf addiction, another's skin ailment. Even if you do come home with a phone number, all you do is stare at it for ten days, mooning over your old flame. What are they up to? Where are they now?

Instead of healing, the big gaping hole in your chest grows larger day by day, as does the pile of advice from friends, family, and know-it-all dating-book authors.

Should you really be out there looking for love or, failing that, lust? Should you just hole up and write bad poetry?

According to the experts, the rhyming dictionary is not a bad way to go. "After you have been hurt in a broken love affair you may want to retreat and nurse your wounds for a while," advises Evelyn Millis Duvall in *The Art of Dating*. "Perhaps taking a breather may do you good."

For Susan, a 31-year-old advertising executive from New York, a breather makes sense.

"I went out with this guy for three years and then, out of the blue, he dumped me," she says. "My friends all told me to go out and just have some fun, to date around. But the thought of sitting across from some guy at a restaurant just makes me want to throw up."

Obviously, Susan's not ready to date. But if we're not supposed to date our way out of the breakup blues, what are we to do instead?

"Try to vitally absorb yourself in something important to you, such as a political movement, a challenging new job, or writing a book," suggests Dr. Albert Ellis, author of *Sex and the Single Man* (1963). "If you can't find a main, overwhelming interest, at least see that your energies are involved in smaller affairs. Play games, attend functions, study some subject, meet new people, take up a hobby or two."

Unfortunately, most of us take a completely different tack.

"So many men and women just jump from relationship to relationship without spending any time alone," writes Robert, a 37-year-old bachelor. "I've been set up on a few blind dates only to find out that the person has only been broken up for a week or so. Maybe that's why relationships aren't successful; people don't take time for themselves."

So how much time should you take?

"The best advice I was ever given was to wait six months after a breakup in order to clear my head and bring myself back together," says Anthony, 26, of Seattle.

*Sex and the City*'s Charlotte claimed it takes half as long as the entire length of the relationship to recover from a breakup. Sociologist and relationship expert Dr. Pepper Schwartz uses a different standard.

# Post-Breakup Dating Tips

Dating after a bad breakup can feel like walking into a raging house fire. It's scary, it's confusing, and you can just about bet you're gonna get burned. But you don't have to, says Dr. Pepper Schwartz, University of Washington sociology professor and author of Finding Your Perfect Match. If you're mindful of your vulnerable state, you'll be able to easily navigate through all that smoke and confusion. Her surefire tips:

**DON'T LOOK TOO NEEDY**, even if you are.

**DON'T LOOK EASY**, in a sexual sense or otherwise. People value that which is special, so show that you value yourself. Don't say "fine" when someone calls and asks you out at 10 p.m.

**BE DISCRIMINATING.** Let people know that they're going to get a piece of you only if they're special.

**RESPECT YOURSELF AND OTHERS.** Make sure that you're treated as valuable and with respect. If someone doesn't return your calls, don't call them again.

**DON'T PUT YOURSELF INTO A PITIFUL SPACE.** It will erode your own estimation of yourself, and that's the best thing you've got. Don't go out there with an attitude of "Why would you go out with me?" because people will just respond with "Yeah, why would I?"

**PUT A GOOD FACE ON YOUR PROBLEMS.** It's hard to do if you're lonely and insecure, but that's your job. Show people that you are worthy, that you're special, and that you have a good life. Show them that sure, you may have *some* problems, but you're not a *bowl* of problems.

"If you still cry at country-and-western songs, then you're not ready to date," she says. "Seriously, if you cry easily at slightly maudlin songs or movies, you're not healed yet. You have to be a reasonably happy person to attract the kind of person you want. If you're unhappy, if you're wounded, then you won't attract anyone except someone as unhappy and as wounded as you are. And that's not a good thing."

The bottom line? Nobody wants to go on a date with the walking wounded. If you feel like crying or fainting or throwing up whenever someone mentions your ex's name, then you probably shouldn't be on the dating circuit, no matter what your buddies tell you. Same goes for those of you who spend all your time talking about how much you miss the smell of your ex's hair while you're out with someone new. Your dates don't want to hear about your old flame's hair. They have hair of their own and it smells pretty good too.

If you've just come out of a star-crossed love affair, grant yourself the gift of an all-important dating time-out. Write the bad poetry. Sing those tortured love songs. Mope. Then mope some more. And when you need to talk out your broken relationship blues, do it with either an understanding friend or a counselor, as *The Art of Dating* advises, or via an online forum (try www. BreakupNews.com for starters). Take your time, take a vacation, or take yoga classes. The important thing is to take yourself— and your vulnerable state—seriously.

"If you've been hurt, cocoon for a while," says Tina Tessina, psychotherapist and author of *The Unofficial Guide to Dating Again* (2002). "Give up the search and stay around trustworthy friends whose presence will soothe you and remind you that you're lovable and likeable. There is a middle ground between going right back out there and getting hurt before you're healed, and hiding alone in your room feeling sorry for yourself. After a short time of being safe with friends, you'll feel strong enough to take another risk."

In other words, you'll be ready to date.

---

## IT'S A MAD MAD MAD MAD WORLD

*Being unstable and bitchy is all part of my mystique.*
—REFRIGERATOR MAGNET, EPHEMERA, INC.

Of course, some people don't get sad—they get mad.

Today's world is chockablock with angry people, and the chips on their shoulders come in all shapes and sizes. Some folks are pissed off at the whole planet. Others hate just half of it, generally the male or the female half. And others focus all of their churning, burning hatred on that one special someone.

"I met this guy through a newspaper's online personals," says Renate, from Santa Fe. "We messaged back and forth and when we met, he seemed great—big smiles all the way around. We ordered drinks and started to chat, and the conversation flowed nicely until he had a few drinks under his belt. Then he busts out with what a fucking bitch his ex-wife was and how happy they were until the fucking whore cheated on him and broke his heart, yada yada yada. He was really loud and people were staring at us. It was awful."

Everybody gets angry sometimes, particularly after a bad breakup. But if you find you're starting to stockpile poisons (metaphorically or otherwise), then you might want to have a little heart-to-heart with your big bad self. According to Pepper Schwartz, a little anger after a romance has gone sour can be a good thing. But too much is asking for trouble.

"You can be angry for a while," says Schwartz. "If you've really been screwed, it's even a healthy reaction. But at some point it hurts no one but you. The question is how long it goes on."

Seething for months—or even years—is a sign that something's just not working.

"If you feel like you have unsolved issues—you're angry at men or you think all women are after your money—if you can't shake them and they're getting in between you and your ability to have a good relationship, that's when you need to go to counseling," she says.

What if you're not the one with the anger problem, but your date is? Then watch out, advises Tina Tessina.

"There's a lot of bad behavior and a bunch of yahoos out there," she says. "People really need to pay attention to who they're dating. Stop being all googly-eyed about how wonderful you think the person is and focus on what's going on. Listen to their conversation; observe how they deal with others. Somebody who yells at a waitress will do it to you sooner or later."

Having a hard time judging whether your date is *too* cranky? Then call in the friend squad.

"It's good for two people who are dating to spend time with friends," says Tessina. "You need to gather input, to know what they think of the person, to help you look for their character, especially if you're looking for something for the long term or looking not to get hurt. If you're just looking for a sport fuck, it doesn't really matter who that person is. But if you're looking to feel cared about and respected, then you need to figure out their character *before* you get involved so you don't have a lot to lose."

Are our friends our only weapon of defense? Not quite. Buried deep within each and every one of us is another sure-fire

# Psycho Chick Checklist

Many psycho chicks aren't aware that other people—particularly their exes—think of them as scary psychotic bitches from hell. So here's a handy checklist to help you figure out whether you're acting just a little abbie-normal or veering toward that dangerous bunny-boiling stage. Check more than one, and you may want to give yourself a dating time-out.

__ Ending a relationship with anything less than a court order is just plain unfriendly.

__ Breaking down your ex-lover's dead-bolted front door is great aerobic exercise.

__ Sleeping in your car outside an ex-lover's house is a fun form of camping.

__ Contacting your ex-lover's work and informing them that he or she has stolen from the company / tried to murder you / is wanted in three states for child molestation is a great prank for April Fool's Day—or any day, for that matter.

__ Going to your ex-lover's parents' house dressed as a cop and telling them their child is dead is very cleansing.

__ Slitting your wrists on the steps of the church while your ex is inside getting married is a unique and memorable wedding gift.

Choose one: My ex still loves me but can't express it because:

    __ He/she's afraid of love.
    __ He/she's afraid of me.
    __ I cut out his/her tongue while he/she was asleep.
    __ All of the above.

# Bitter Guy Guidelines

Oftentimes, bitter men don't realize that all their venomous venting serves only to drive away potential dates—usually at breakneck speed. Concerned that your bitter baggage is starting to reach the steamer trunk stage? Then take a look at these handy guidelines. If you check more than one, it's time to give that overworked spleen a rest!

__ Standing some bitch up on a first date is a great way to let her know right off the bat that you're not going to deal with any of her high-maintenance crap.

__ Never miss an opportunity to accuse a woman of being a gold-digging tramp—it keeps them on their toes.

__ Posting doctored photos of your ex having sex with various barnyard animals is a great way to soothe your savage beast.

__ If a woman offers to pick up the check on a date, she's only trying to undermine your manhood.

__ A woman who brings you homemade chicken soup when you're sick is hoping to case your house while you're too weak to stop her.

__ Show me a woman who's forgotten to take her birth control pill and I'll show you a woman who's trying to get pregnant in order to collect child support.

Choose one: If a woman fails to answer the phone when you call, it's because:

    __ The goddamn bitch is sleeping with your best friend.
    __ The goddamn bitch is sleeping with your boss.
    __ The goddamn bitch is sleeping.
    __ All of the above.

yahoo alarm, which if you're paying attention will help you distinguish the stinkers from the stars. What is this secret alarm system? It's called your gut, as Nick, a 56-year-old Seattle single, can tell you.

### Dysfunctional Parking Only

*I met John through an online gay chat line and we made a date for coffee. How civilized, I thought. He picked me up on a Saturday morning, and we headed to a Starbucks at a nearby shopping mall. Unfortunately, when we got there, every parking place was taken. We circled through the parking lot for ten, fifteen, twenty minutes. Finally, he saw a van's rear lights go on and sped up to get the spot. Another car saw the van leaving, too, though, and headed straight for it. My date laid on the horn, a woman got out of the other car, and they immediately started shouting at each other. Then the shouting got really nasty. John called her a bitch; she called him an asshole. Then she spread her arms like a human blockade and he threatened to run her over. By then, I no longer wanted coffee—or anything else to do with this man. So I jumped out of the car and headed for home. Looking back, I saw the van hightailing it out of there, too, revealing that the parking space was for disabled people only.*

Granted, some volatile people may come off as exciting and/ or passionate to the uninitiated—all that fire! all that music! all those crazy antics! Bob, a 26-year-old bachelor from Vermont, finds his girlfriend's histrionic behavior downright exhilarating. "There's been drunken yelling, crying, vomiting, biting, jumping out of cars, running away—you name it," he says. "But one of the reasons I like her is that she's very feisty."

But sometimes all that feistiness can be indicative of something else—i.e., your date is nuts. If you're dating someone who starts exhibiting signs of mental instability (they break into your car and pee on the seat when you forget to call them), chances are it won't be long before all that exciting fire and music explodes in your face. Just ask Rhett, a thirtysomething single from Seattle.

### That Instant Electricity

*I was living with this girl—we'd known each other about three months when she moved in—and she desperately wanted to get married. I wasn't ready to get married, though, and this made her pretty angry, I guess. One night I came home from work and found our place completely dark. When I reached around to turn on the light switch, there was nothing there. She'd taken off the switch plate and the wires were all exposed. She'd done that throughout the entire place. All the switch plates were off, but the power was still on. I guess she was trying to kill me or something.*

Obviously, abusive dates are no laughing matter. But unfortunately, they *are* out there, and part of being ready to date is learning to recognize these losers when you stumble onto them. If you've accidentally become involved with someone who exhibits abusive behavior or who makes the hair on the back of your neck stand up in a creepy way, move on and fast.

And if *you're* the one who can't let go of the anger, who's seething over the way your ex broke up with you *years* after the fact, then do yourself and all those poor saps you keep bad-mouthing a favor and seek professional help. Check that bitter baggage at the therapist's door before you try to jump back on the love train. Your friends will thank you, your future dates will thank you— and your healthy heart and winning personality will eventually thank you too.

## EMOTIONAL ODDS AND ENDS

*I will not fall for any of the following: alcoholics, work-aholics, commitment phobics, people with girlfriends or wives, misogynists, megalomaniacs, chauvinists, fuck-wits or freeloaders, perverts.*

—HELEN FIELDING,
*BRIDGET JONES'S DIARY*, 1996

Are there other reasons why people may not be ready to date? Only about a million and a half. Some of us have commitment issues—news flash! yes, both men *and* women. Others have trouble dealing with rejection. And then there are those suffering from addictions—alcohol, drugs, gambling, food, sex—any of which can wreak havoc on a person's dating life.

"I met this girl online who said she loved great food and wine," says John, a 33-year-old bachelor from New York. "She was attractive, educated, funny—the complete package. We decided to go out to dinner to this nice Italian restaurant, but as soon as we started ordering and eating, it became obvious something was up. She ate two appetizers, then an entire loaf of bread. Then a plate of anti-pasto, followed by more bread, a plate of pasta, a whole fish, and not one but two entrees. She must have excused herself to go to the restroom three times during the meal; and by the end of the evening, the entire waitstaff was talking about her freakish behavior. I was totally turned off, but it was also sort of fascinating—like watching a train wreck."

Does the fact that you have an eating disorder mean you should get out of the dating pool? Not necessarily.

"If you have a problem—and a lot of people are in denial about their addiction problems—you may want to just meet with people who are in recovery like yourself," says Tina Tessina. "That way, you'll be in a social group and you'll be able to learn from other experiences and mistakes."

Social groups and support networks are important for all of us when it comes to emotional health, says Tessina, especially when we're dating.

"If you partake in some kind of bad behavior, your social network will let you know; they'll give you feedback," she says. "And if your date is doing something weird behind your back, they'll tell you that too."

What kind of weird things could a date do? How much time do you have?

"Twenty-five percent of the population has some significant emotional problem that will get in the way of relationships," says Dr. Roy Lubit, psychiatrist with the Center for Social and Emotional Education and author of *Coping with Toxic Managers and Subordinates and Other Difficult People in Your Life* (2003). Psychiatrists use terms like "narcissistic," "histrionic," and "borderline personality" to describe a few of these folks—but you may simply know them as the boyfriend or girlfriend from hell. Unfortunately, some of us are so tired of being alone that we're willing to overlook a few quirky behaviors—you know, little things like pervasive bouts of lying, cheating, and armed robbery—just so we'll have a warm body next to us at night.

"A lot of people are really desperate, so they'll ignore warning signs," says Tessina.

Don't do this. Also, don't try to rescue them. And most important of all, don't let them get under your skin—a difficult task, since many of these folks can be très charming. What can you do instead? Keep your perspective. And definitely keep friends close at hand.

"I started dating this guy I met at a coffeehouse, shortly after returning from a teaching position in South America," says Donna, a 34-year-old single from Sacramento. "He was unassuming and friendly and on our second date, he told me he'd lost his wife in a snowmobiling accident. I told a friend about him, and she said she'd seen some articles in the paper about a man who was being sued by his former in-laws. Apparently, they were suspicious about the circumstances surrounding the death of their daughter—who had died in a snowmobiling accident. I did some research and it turned out to be the same man. I broke things off with him, and the following spring, he was arrested and stood trial for murder."

Tessina says good friends can be crucial when it comes to warding off toxic dates—as can paying close attention to those all-important red flags, which you'll find discussed ad nauseam in any self-help aisle in the country. Remember: An important part of being ready to date is knowing who you need to *avoid*.

All of us have to deal with emotional upheaval now and again. Death, divorce, bankruptcy, irritable bowel syndrome—you never know what might come knocking on your front door, sending your lovely, secure life to hell in a handbasket. Some people may look for solace from their troubles in countless pints of Hefeweizen or Häagen-Dazs. Still others may try to use a new lover to fill that big gaping hole where their self-esteem used to be.

How you deal with life's challenges is up to you. But until you *do* deal with emotional pitfalls, putting yourself through a hodgepodge of dating experiences may only complicate matters.

So before you jump into the dating pool, take a good long look in the mirror and check to see if you've got a bit of spinach in your teeth or a few flecks of dandruff on your jacket, emotionally speaking, of course. If you do, consider getting yourself some psychological Head & Shoulders (and feel free to pass a complimentary bottle to those you meet along the way). It's all part of the process of getting yourself ready to date.

## AND LET'S NOT FORGET SOCIAL SKILLS

*Oh, behave!*
            —*Austin Powers: International Man of Mystery*, 1997

Some would argue that basic social skills don't exist anymore. And truly, why should they? Between our email and voice mail, BlackBerries and laptops, IMs and iPods, we rarely need to speak to one another in person. Is it any surprise that some of us have forgotten how to relate to others without keyboard emoticons? LOL!

Unless you want to spend all of your time with a virtual boyfriend or girlfriend (and yes, these do exist, courtesy of a company called Artificial Life), knowing how to relate to others in real time is key.

"Manners and social skills are still required when it comes to dating," says Kellie, a 44-year-old Seattle single. "The women's movement, the sexual revolution, AIDS, et cetera, have changed a lot of things. But what's at the core has remained intact."

And what *is* at the core of dating? The same thing that's at the core of all other social interaction: etiquette.

What does that mean? It means knowing how to conduct a conversation without offending everyone within earshot. Knowing how to eat a meal in public without mortifying your mother. Being respectful of privacy—yours as well as others'. Not picking fights. Not picking your nose. Not getting drunk and making an ass of yourself in public. In general, it means behaving yourself—not in a snooty "that's the oyster fork, you imbecile" manner, but in a socially acceptable, considerate way that will enable you to smoothly navigate any setting, table or otherwise.

"Etiquette . . . is concerned with those rules of the 'game of life' which make it easier and simpler for us to mingle with one another," writes Lillian Eichler in *Today's Etiquette* (1940).

So with mingling in mind, let's turn to these few thoughts.

## THE ART OF CONVERSATION

*You've heard it again and again: to be popular, be a good listener. Yes, [even] the most brilliant monologue becomes tiresome. In order to make friends and attract people, you must pay attention to them.*

—SALLY SIMPSON,
*POPULARITY PLUS*, 1950

Do you give good voice? Can you talk about anything—or, more importantly, nothing—with humor, charm, and appeal? If so, you're blessed, because for you there will never be any of those awkward chasms that can open up in the middle of a conversation, swallowing up your hopes for a fascinating exchange like so many tossed rocks. Unfortunately, the art of conversation doesn't come easily for everybody. Some of us are shy or reserved; others blather on incessantly about everything from our impending bankruptcy to the butt boil our cousin got down in Mexico.

Is this conversation? Maybe yes, maybe no. If the person you're talking to is just as enthusiastic about butt boils as you are, then you're fine. But if they're squirming uncomfortably while you launch into the gory details of the lancing, then that's not so much a conversation as an exercise in torture. Why? Because a good conversation is a partnership.

## IT'S ALL ABOUT GIVE-AND-TAKE

"Think of conversation as a bridge to link two personalities brought together for a moment by the tide of life," writes Lady Troubridge in *Etiquette and Entertaining to Help You on Your Social Way* (circa 1920).

If you want to attract a date, you have to know how to communicate. Which means you have to know how to cross that all-important conversational bridge, as Rachel, a 35-year-old communications specialist from Seattle, can tell you.

### *Mr. Monosyllable*

*I met this guy at a speed-dating event. Apparently, his brother had convinced him to go because he'd met the love of his life during a speed-dating session and had just gotten married to the woman. My guess, though, is that the brother had a few more social skills than the guy I met. This guy was so shy, and so nervous, that he could barely get even one-word answers out. It made for a really engrossing six minutes. I suppose I should support him for making the effort, but I won't be the one dating him.*

Conversation is all about give-and-take. When someone asks you a question, they're dowsing around for a topic that the two of you can discuss with interest, enthusiasm, aplomb. It's a dance, and if one partner refuses to move their feet, then all action stops right there.

"If you find yourself at the receiving end of a group of exploratory questions, do not limit your answers to monosyllables," advises the author of *How to Get Along with Girls* (1944). "Be cooperative. Men sometimes lose out at the very beginning because girls find them so hard to talk to."

The truth is, everyone loses out when you can't keep a conversation going.

"A lot of the guys I meet tend to have really poor dating skills," says Ken, a 38-year-old single from Seattle. "Just basic 101 kind of stuff. You meet, you introduce yourself, you talk about the usual stuff, you ask questions, and some of these guys won't answer. They're missing the basic skills—be polite, ask and answer questions, make eye contact. It doesn't matter if you're gay or straight, these are just basic dating techniques."

## THE CONVERSATIONALLY IMPAIRED

Sometimes, of course, it's not getting people to *open* up, it's getting them to *shut* up. Just ask Margaret, a 24-year-old bachelor girl from Washington, D.C.

### Professor Know-It-All

*I caught the eye of a tall, good-looking guy at a bar one night. We started chatting but the music was so loud I couldn't hear a word he said. He seemed nice, though, so I gave him my number, and he called the next day and asked me out. We went to dinner but by the time the check came, I knew he was not for me. Turtleneck, blazer, laughing at inappropriate times, his legs crossed— it was like being on a date with my math professor. Plus he kept talking about how much dinner cost and how much his law school payments were. I told him I needed to join some friends in a nearby bar in an effort to bail, but he invited himself along. When we got there, the guy literally took over every conversation*

*no matter what the subject. Plus he kept making fun of each of
my friends, where they went to school, their jobs, everything. By
the end, I could tell they all wanted his head on a plate.*

Boorishness is just one type of social sin—there are countless
more. There's Ms. Sentence Finisher, who never lets you complete
a thought—or a story—on your own. Or Mr. One-Upmanship, who
trumps your every tale with his own bigger, better accomplish-
ment. There's the smart-ass who cracks wise with every remark,
and the name-dropper who sprinkles her stories with first-name
references to D-list celebrities. There's Mumbles and the Long-
Winded Wonder and Miss Mouthful, a lovely young woman who
wouldn't dream of swallowing . . . before she starts talking.

And then, of course, there's everybody's favorite—good old
TMI Guy.

"I was asked out by this guy that I'd been talking to [on
the phone] for about a month," writes an anonymous poster on
GirlPosse.com. "We went to a movie and then decided to have dinner afterwards at my favorite pizza place. And while we're waiting
for our order to be taken, he told me all about his spastic colon!"

Of course, there are plenty of TMI Girls out there too, many
of whom feel compelled to share stunningly detailed accounts of
their financial troubles, their sexually transmitted diseases, or
their bouts with depression—all on a first date.

"Whip out your Zoloft bottle and spend an hour and a half
talking about your problems and the side effects of the drugs,
and you won't be seeing me again," says Clayton, 32, of Seattle.
"I'm your date, not your shrink."

Think sharing your mental health history is bad?

"I went out to lunch with this guy at work who had made
it pretty obvious that he had a crush on me, and as we're sitting there eating, he starts talking about his small penis," says
Samantha, a 33-year-old single from Baltimore. "I wasn't that

compelled to go out with him before, but after he slapped out the small penis—come on!"

Butt boils, spastic colons, mental illness, pre-nups—these are just the kind of conversational faux pas that can turn you into a one-date—or no-date—wonder. Are there other conversational landmines? Naturally. Hot topics like politics, religion, or the proper way to hang a roll of toilet paper are always good for few fireworks.

"I met this girl through mutual friends and we went out to get a bite to eat," says Todd, a 36-year-old bartender from Seattle. "And she started talking politics. I tried to circumvent any kind of political discussion—I knew that some of my views might not mesh with hers—but she just kept at me and at me. We finally ended up getting into a discussion about labor and minimum wage. I said I thought the minimum wage was too high—and she threw a beer on me."

Do try to learn how to hold a discussion—or a debate—without resorting to fisticuffs, metaphorical or otherwise. Another important quality to master: sensitivity.

"I had a date with this guy—a friend of a friend," says Diane, 44. "I wanted to cancel because I'd had to put down a family pet the day before, but I pulled myself together and went out to meet him. I was really off my mark, but realized halfway through the date that the guy wouldn't have noticed if I'd been in a coma. He talked about himself incessantly and when he wasn't doing that, he was badmouthing his co-workers, his former employers, his friends (including the one who set us up). After a while, I began to wish I could have put *him* down."

## THE CONVERSATION MUST GO ON

Blowhards, brick walls, fight pickers, gossips. Soft talkers, nervous twitchers, baggage unpackers, dolts. At one point or another, we all find that we're using crayons when it comes to the fine art of conversation. But neither Rome nor clever repartee was built in a day. Good conversational skills take time to acquire, and half the secret is knowing when to keep your trap shut.

But don't keep it shut too long. Conversation is a dance, which means everybody needs to keep their feet moving. They talk, then you talk. They ask questions, then you ask questions. The pendulum swings back and forth, back and forth, like seventh-graders doing a slow dance. And speaking of slow, if you feel that your conversations lag, make an effort to get out into the world so you have more to contribute. Read the best sellers, watch the news, peruse the magazine stands, the museums, the farmer's markets. Visit Madagascar, if you have to.

Be informed, be polite, and be ready to share your airspace with another, particularly if you're interested in sharing something more—a meal, a movie, a bed—down the road. Practice your speaking skills with others (yes, I'm talking about holding conversations with people you may not actually want to sleep with), then spend even more time learning how to *listen*, perhaps the most valuable social skill of all.

# GOOD MANNERS ARE ESSENTIAL

*The greatest asset that a man or woman or even a child can have is charm. And charm cannot exist without good manners.*

—Emily Post,
*Etiquette*, 1942

Quick question: If a woman gets up from a table at a restaurant, is the man she's sitting with ill-mannered if he doesn't stand? The answer: Who knows? The important thing is that he doesn't slap her on the ass as she walks by or start putting the moves on the hottie at the next table while she's gone. In other words, dating manners are not what they used to be.

In fact, manners in general have been on a slow and steady decline for years—just ask anyone who's had six people show up for a dinner party without RSVPing or who's watched a beautiful young woman nonchalantly pick her nose while waiting at a stoplight.

## WHO KILLED EMILY POST?

Why have our manners gone missing? For a number of reasons, according to Peter Post, grandson of Emily Post and author of several etiquette books, including *Essential Manners for Men* (2003) and *Essential Manners for Couples* (2005).

"People growing up in the '60s, '70s, and '80s grew up in a 'me-ism' world, where 'I'm what's important, not you,'" says Post. "The general attitude became 'I can do things the way I want and if you don't like it, tough.'"

And then, along came technology with its instant-gratification mind-set.

"The speed with which things happen is much faster today," says Post. "Everything's instant. We all have to be available 24/7. We no longer sit back and consider 'Is this the right thing to say? How am I handling myself?' There's no time for that."

As a result, people have found little time to practice good manners, if they've even learned them at all. "If you think about where you learn your manners, it's usually from your parents," says Post. "But we no longer have that nuclear family with Mom at home and Dad out working. Today, we have both parents working, single-parent families, even no-parent families. If you're not around people who teach you manners, you don't learn them."

In other words, we've all grown up in a perfect storm of mannerlessness. The inevitable result?

"We have people coming out of college who may have job skills, but they don't know how to hold a fork," says Post. "They've just never learned their basic social graces. They aren't sure what to do."

Which may just be a gracious way of saying we've all become a bunch of rude jerks. Or, at least some of us have, such as this fellow that Sally, a 50-year-old single from Brooklyn, met not long ago.

### Museum of Bad Manners

*I started corresponding with a man via the Internet who described himself as very educated, well read, and attractive, and I decided to meet him at a museum show in Brooklyn. We met, strolled around, and everything was fine until he started lecturing me on every exhibit, to the point where I couldn't get in two words edgewise. Then he chastised me for touching some of the furniture, claiming it would ruin the patina of the wood. (The furniture was not enclosed in a glass case or anything, and I certainly wasn't manhandling it.) The corker, though, was when he pushed aside a little girl who was using a computer by an exhibit we were looking at. He claimed he'd been there first. I wanted to die of mortification.*

Bullying small children is not only the height of bad behavior, it's also the absolute worst way to impress a date, unless you're trying to impress them with what a jackass you are. Luckily, not everyone's manners are that far gone. But we do have our moments.

## FIRST DATE OR LAST DATE?

"One time on a date this guy picked up his cell phone and called his brother while I was midsentence," says Sonia, a 29-year-old product manager from Seattle.

"I went to dinner with this guy who started chatting up the woman at the next table right in front of me," says Chrissie, a singleton from Bridlington, England.

Jean-Pierre's date was so rude to the waitstaff at a restaurant that halfway through the meal he paid for the dinner, gave her cab fare, and left. Susan's date kept her waiting in his living room for an hour while he made phone calls, then came out and asked her to take off her clothes so they could go to bed. Both Teresa and Allan met people for dates, only to discover that their dates brought dates *with* them. And poor Diane in San Francisco actually went out with a man who peed in her neighbor's yard—in broad daylight!

What do these stories have in common? They all happened on first dates, when people traditionally display their very best behavior.

Whether our civility has been sacrificed at the altar of cyberspace or has been swapped out for that all-too-necessary second parental income, it's evident that consideration for others is diminishing with time. According to a survey of 847 people conducted by the Emily Post Institute, 81 percent felt society was far more uncivil today than it was twenty years ago, citing lack of respect, lack of consideration, lack of patience, callousness, selfishness, and intolerance for others as the prime culprits.

"Once I went on a blind date with this woman I'd talked to for

# Take This Date and Shove It

Some people equate finding a boyfriend or girlfriend with finding a job. After all, both provide security, interpersonal interaction, and according to some studies, health benefits. And if relationships are jobs, it follows that the first date is the job interview. Have you become a one-date wonder, flitting from one person's company to the next? Then perhaps you should study this list of why people don't get hired:

- Poor personal appearance
- Failure to make eye contact
- Lack of enthusiasm
- Vague responses
- Lack of poise
- Overemphasis on money
- Condemns past employers
- Shows no interest in the company
- Doesn't ask questions
- Inarticulate
- Discourtesy
- Makes excuses
- Lacks goals
- Arrives late
- Little sense of humor
- Lacks maturity
- Overbearing
- Narrow interests
- Limp handshake

—COURTESY OF SHERRI EDWARDS,
RESOURCEMAXIMIZER.COM

about four hours on the phone," says Manuel, a 32-year-old single from Philadelphia. "She invited me to a concert, very spur of the moment. And afterward, instead of dropping me at the train station, she insisted on driving me home. Only I guess it took her longer than she expected, because she suddenly stopped the car in the middle of nowhere and asked me to get out and walk the rest of the way. It was a cold February night, around midnight. I couldn't comprehend that anyone could be that selfish and rude."

But people *are* that selfish and rude, especially when it comes to dating. They're also thoughtless, inconsiderate, discourteous, and unbelievably presumptuous. Sometimes intentionally, other times because they simply don't know any better. Not that this is much of an excuse when there are hundreds of books, Web sites, and newspaper columns (hooray for Miss Manners!) dedicated to all things etiquette, a word which in and of itself can cause women to sweat, children to twitch, and men to suffer shrinkage.

## THE E-WORD

Perhaps it's this fear of the e-word itself that causes us to shun its practice. Etiquette brings to mind finger bowls, calling cards, and towers of starched white linen. It conjures up nightmares of musty rooms filled with parchment-faced people, half of whom are wearing monocles and the other half of whom are dead. But as much as we'd like to bury old etiquette before its time, its principles are alive and well—at least in our heart of hearts. Because at its core, etiquette is simply about treating people with consideration, respect, and honesty—and truly, isn't that what we all want from each other, *especially* when we're dating?

"A date is wholly satisfying only when each person is considerate of the other," writes Evelyn Millis Duvall in *The Art of Dating*. "Dating is not fun if either of you flirts conspicuously with others, brags about previous conquests, gossips about other dates . . . avoids participation in the activities or makes an issue over minor mishaps. Such behavior is essentially a lack of courtesy and it can really keep you from enjoying each other."

Good words to live by. I'd add the following:

Be on time. Don't stand people up unless there's some kind of emergency, and then make sure you let them know what's happened. Say please and thank you when people do nice things for you, like opening a door, buying a meal, or complimenting you on your outfit (incidentally, "Nice ass" is not a respectful way to compliment someone's outfit). Don't lead someone on just to be nice. Don't pick your teeth (or anything else, for that matter) at the table. Be polite to the waitstaff at restaurants. Never shout, "You still live with your mother?" in a crowded coffee shop. Don't belittle anyone for not knowing Cal Ripken's lifetime RBI record or verbally castrate them if they can't remember where they parked their car, even if you are wearing really really high heels.

Don't tell someone they're pretty for a fat girl (or boy). Learn how to use silverware. Don't gouge people for free meals or free drinks. Respect people's privacy. If they don't want to talk about their ex-boyfriend, their skin condition, their experiences in Iraq, or why they're deathly afraid of mimes, don't badger them. If you go to a party with one person, don't end up having sex with someone else in the back room, unless it's that kind of party and the two of you have discussed the possibility beforehand. Don't smoke if the person you're with has asked you not to. Do laugh at people's jokes.

One final tip: Don't ask people to touch your private parts if you've only known them for a matter of minutes.

"I met this guy through the Internet and five minutes after we met, he asked me to touch his penis," writes Sally from Brooklyn. "He said he asks *all* women he meets to do this. It was the shortest date I ever had."

Don't let *your* shortcomings in the, um, manners department be what people remember most about you. Be polite, folks.

# PART TWO

# HOW TO FIND A DATE

*Obviously you will not meet a man by sitting at home. Circulate where there are men. There may be opportunities in your office or factory—use them. Attend your union meetings. Volunteer for committee work. Join a political party, a club, a class, a church group. Keep active and you are bound to meet men.*

—W. S. KEATING,
*HOW TO GET ALONG WITH BOYS,* 1945

# WHY DO YOU WANT TO DATE?

*The female is eager to cultivate the friendship of men for admirable reasons: One, to acquire a husband. Two, practically nothing that is any fun can be done without a male escort. Men, however, do not seek feminine companionship for the pure enjoyment of conversation, dancing, picnics, marriage, and other innocent pleasures. Regrettably, they have something else in mind.*

—NINA FAREWELL,
*THE UNFAIR SEX*, 1953

Why do you want to date? Some people, for instance those frantic women who devour every fifteen-step "how-to-catch-a-manual" to hit the bookshelves, date because they want to get married—*now*. Others are looking for something less permanent: some casual conversation, some casual sex.

For 23-year-old Mark, it's not just sex—it's *good* sex. "Anybody can have a one-night stand. But sex definitely gets better over time if it's with the right person."

Desiree, 48, is in it for the sex as well, although she does own up to a bit of a mixed agenda. "I love being with men and I really like sex," she says, "but as much as I hate to admit it, underneath it all, I'm still looking for that freaking picket fence."

For 30-year-old Michael, it's friendship. For Eric, 27, free meals. Jean-Pierre, 46, is searching for his soul mate. Jesse, 27, some companionship and making out. Some folks date out of boredom, others out of spite.

"I once had a friend who would do that," writes Carly, a 40-year-old from Jersey City. "If a guy tried to pick her up on the street in an unflattering way, she'd date him for spite and make his night miserable just to teach him a lesson."

Whether it's free food, family pressure, or a potential 401k, everybody dates for a reason. The tricky part is finding someone whose reason is reasonably close to yours.

"I wish everyone could wear a sign stating their intentions," says Karen, a 31-year-old teacher from Chicago. "That way, those looking to just hook up could find each other, have sex, and be happy. And those of us who want something a little more substantial could zero in on the right people."

Her solution?

"Remember Garanimals? Everything with a giraffe tag went together, or a panda tag, et cetera. You didn't have to worry about matching; you could tell just by looking. We need those tags."

Unfortunately, we don't have those tags. And even if we did, there would still be problems. Why? Because people are not always entirely forthcoming about their motives, particularly when it comes to love and/or lust. Even if a tag clearly reads Friends with Benefits, the person may actually be a Wannabe Wife.

So how do we draw a clear bead on our date's dating agenda without resorting to a private investigator and/or a cattle prod? And more than that—how do we know our *own* agenda? We may be absolutely convinced that we're looking for an LTR, when it's really some STF (short-term fun) that we crave.

"I don't know what's wrong with me," sighs Robert, 38. "I thought I really cared about this woman I was seeing, but then I just got bored with her after a few weeks. It seems like I do that a lot."

According to Dr. Pepper Schwartz, it's all about paying attention to the signals.

"People often listen to what other people say, but they don't watch what they do," she says. "They'll find huge ways to excuse behavior—'Oh, he's still hurt' or 'Oh, he doesn't want to spend

# What's Your Dating Tag?

We're all familiar with serial daters and cyber-upgraders, but there are other dating types lurking around Out There. Which one are you?

**THE SAMPLER:** Just like those nonstop noshers who stroll through the grocery store sampling every bit of free Brie that's put before them, the Sampler is compelled to snack on American singles for the rest of his or her life. They're out for a Gouda time—and nothing more. While everybody loves a variety pack, remember that too much snacking can ruin your appetite—for love.

**THE SEARCHER:** To the Searcher; you're either marriage material or you're a waste of time. And for Searchers, it's all about time, which might explain that loud ticking sound you hear whenever you're around one. Does the person you're with make you feel more like you're on an interview than a date? Do they routinely bring up phrases like commitment-phobe, soul mate, or princess cut? No worries if the answer's yes. Fail to pony up that "I do" and your Searcher will be back on the trail in no time.

**THE INSTA-SPOUSE:** Like the Searcher, this single is interested in getting married, only they don't necessarily need a ring or a wedding ceremony. Dinner, coffee, or even a friendly email exchange is enough to convince them you're a couple. How can you spot an Insta-Spouse? Simple. Just check your cell phone, your email, or your rearview mirror. They're there—24/7.

**THE SECRET SHOPPER:** Like the Searcher, the Secret Shopper may seem to have an endless array of interview questions, but they're not searching for a spouse as much as a reason to scratch you off their list. How can you spot a Secret Shopper? Look for their gigantic clipboard full of 1,001 necessary requirements—or listen for the unmistakable sense of entitlement. "I wouldn't *dream* of dating anyone without an income of $500K. Why should *I* settle?" If all else fails, watch for the telltale limp—these folks have definitely shot themselves in the relationship foot.

**THE VULTURE:** You're sitting at the bar, shell-shocked from a sudden bust-up, when you suddenly hear the flap of wings, smell the faint odor of carrion (or is that Tag body spray?), and look up to find yourself face-to-face with a Vulture. Ever on the prowl, a Vulture can pick up the scent of relationship roadkill miles away. Why? Because they prefer to live off the grisly remains of a dead affair rather than starting something new themselves. Beware!

**THE AMAZING DISAPPEAR-O:** You've had six weeks of blissful togetherness when suddenly your new love comes down with a cold or gets super slammed at work. And presto-chango! They're gone. *Where* did they go? *Why* did they go? You'll never know—their motivations remain a dark, disturbing riddle. But don't despair. The Amazing Disappear-O cannot be understood by mere mortals—they are inscrutable, they are unfathomable, they are an enigma wrapped in a mystery and covered with a huge layer of chickenshit. Move on. They have.

the holidays with me because he wants to be with his mother at Christmas'—all kinds of garbage. If somebody isn't looking for a relationship, it shows up over time."

In fact, Schwartz says all dating agendas become evident in time.

"If somebody says they're just looking for fun, but they're really upset that you can't go out on a Saturday night, it's obviously not just all about having fun," she says. "Take your cues from people's behavior; that's what's going to tell you what their agenda is. It's not what they say—'I'm a free spirit' or 'I'm looking for the love of my life'—it's what they do."

But where do you find these like-minded sorts? The bookstore? The blues club? The board meeting? It all depends on what you're looking for. If an hour or two of sloppy kissing is your goal, then the local cocktail lounge should do just fine. If it's casual dating with tons of different people that you crave, then an Internet dating site or a night of speed dating is probably your best bet. Marriage more your scene? Then chances are a matchmaker or a good old-fashioned setup or eHarmony is a better option.

*Why* you want to date naturally determines *how* you go about finding one.

# CHAPTER 3

# GOOD OLD-FASHIONED FREE LOVE

*Every day and every night, thousands of girls sit in offices, go to parties, wait for elevators to come and lights to change, buckle their airplane seat belts, and strap-hang on subways, and look wistfully at the princes, near princes, and knaves they cannot quite start conversations with.*

—Helen Gurley Brown, Editor,
*The Cosmo Girl's Guide to the New Etiquette*, 1971

Way back in the dark ages of dating (you know, before the Internet), most people picked up a date the same way they picked up a bad cold—either a friend, family member, or co-worker was responsible, or they simply stumbled onto it in the street. These days, things are a little different. Strangers rarely speak to one another on the street or the coffee shop or the commuter train, either out of fear, shyness, disdain, or because they're already involved in a long-term relationship with their cell phone.

And dating at work is equally problematic. Not only is it risky from a professional standpoint (reason for leaving: got caught fucking in the supply closet), many companies have instituted strict "'no dating'" policies. As have countless singles after enduring one too many setups with Throat-Clearing Girl or Enormous

Head Guy, courtesy of their seemingly insane married friends.

Between life's distractions—technological and otherwise—and the ever-growing array of shiny new dating options, few people give much thought to the old-fashioned methods of meeting. In fact, most of us would just as soon pour out our hearts to some faceless cyberstranger than strike up a conversation with that cute guy or girl standing three feet away from us at the bookstore.

Why? Because we're chicken. And, well, lazy.

"Meeting people online is low risk, plus you can do it in your bathrobe," says Jodi O'Brien, a Seattle University sociologist specializing in gender and sexuality. "You can eat your dinner, wear your comfy clothes, and still meet all sorts of new people. Also, in face-to-face interactions, it's difficult to walk away from someone we don't like. Online, it's easier to control the situation so it's comfortable."

Unfortunately, all this comfort comes with a cost.

"I do think online interaction erodes face-to-face courtship," says O'Brien. "The art of flirting gets lost."

So how do you meet someone without an online profile, a three-minute speed date, or an electronic wink? Read on.

## AT HOME

*Carry a "conversation starter." This is a physical item that is designed to prompt curiosity and provoke interaction. You take it everywhere to trigger spontaneous conversations with interesting strangers. The idea is that a man might see your conversation starter and have an easier time initiating contact with you.*

—Rachel Greenwald,
*Find a Husband After 35 Using What I Learned at Harvard Business School,* 2003

Truth be told, our social backyards are full of potential dates, yet as far as we're concerned, they're all a bunch of noxious weeds. Why? Because we don't like to accept help when it comes to dating. And we also don't want to go out with somebody once and then have to keep looking at their sappy hopeful face every time we show up at a neighborhood barbecue. And most of all, we don't want to go out with somebody we already sort of know.

**FUN FACT:** Researchers at the University of Chicago found that people were twice as likely to meet a date through friends and famlly than through the bar scene.

We want to go out with the Mysterious Stranger—the girl who saves us from the falling piano, the guy who fends off the attacking alien—somebody we've met through the *usual* channels, you know, the way people meet in the movies.

It's much more glamorous to fall in love with the guy who defended you when you were wrongly accused of murder than to fall in love with the guy who delivered your new refrigerator. But it doesn't happen in real life. What does happen? Ask Sarah, 31, from Seattle.

### Revenge of the Singles Table

*I was at the reception for my cousin's wedding and was sick with a cold and at my limit with relatives and small talk. In fact, I was trying to figure out how I could escape the dinner and head for the hotel spa. My cousin put me at a table with all the other leftovers—single-people-who-don't-fit-in-anywhere—and I ended up sitting next to my cousin's husband's cousin. I thought he was cute, but since he was an undergraduate in college (I'm 31) and lived in Connecticut, I didn't expect much. After dinner, though, we started talking—about everything from marital expectations to the cultural implications of* Seinfeld. *In the midst of this intense conversation, our cousins kept dragging us out to the dance floor for the chicken dance, the Locomotion, and other Midwestern wedding favorites. And the evening turned out to be a blast. When I got back home, there was an email waiting for me. Five months later, we're still together.*

## RELEASE YOUR INNER FLIRT

But what do you do if you *don't* happen to be part of a huge social network of friends and meddling family members? Or you've already cut a swath through your entire social circle? Or you just moved to a new city?

Well, open your eyes and look around. Half the country is single (49.6 percent of all households, according to an August 2004 census report), so you can pretty much figure that at least half of the people around you are too. Unfortunately, the first thing most of us do when we spot someone we'd like to meet is walk right up and . . . avoid them. After all, they're probably seeing someone. Or they're married. With a couple of kids. And a huge drinking problem. And debt—lots and lots of debt.

"Instead of making an attempt to flirt with people they're attracted to, most people will just make a list of excuses," says David Wygant, author of *Always Talk to Strangers* (2005). "A woman will be in line at a Starbucks and she'll spot a good-looking guy, but instead of talking to him, she'll say, 'Oh, he looks busy, he's probably married, he may be unstable.' People will look for every possible excuse just to make themselves feel better for not taking a chance."

Why? Because we're wimps.

"Everybody suffers from the same disease," says Wygant. "Everybody has this fear of strangers. But strangers are the ones who hold the key to your dating future."

Rather than freezing people out, Wygant suggests finding some small way to flirt with them instead. In fact, he promotes flirting with everyone and everything we come in contact with—men, women, children, even pets. Does that mean we all have to go out there and start doing the *Legally Blonde* "bend and snap"? Or turn into relentless mate-hunting machines?

Not at all. It just means we need to pull that antisocial stick out of our ass—at least partway.

"People need to lighten up, start smiling at each other," says Wygant. "They need to go out there and do some verbal batting practice."

When and where should we be doing all this practice? Everywhere. Everywhen.

Interesting people are all over. They're at the coffee shop in the morning, the dry cleaner's in the afternoon. They're sitting one booth over at our favorite Thai place, or waiting for us to finish our biceps curls at the gym. They're pumping gas next to us, buying toilet paper behind us. They may even be checking out your ass as you read this page.

What do you have to do to meet one of these people? Try acknowledging their presence, for starters. Make eye contact. Smile and say hello. Ask them what time it is. If they think it's going to rain. If they know if the food at the new Italian place down the street is any good. If their dog bites. You don't need to sacrifice your dignity or employ vast amounts of subterfuge; just drop some form of metaphorical hankie (along with that ubiquitous antisocial stance). Engage with them in a nonthreatening and—if you can pull it off—charming manner. If all else fails, just do what this woman did to meet Kent, a fortysomething single from Seattle.

### Bus Stop

*Every day I ride a train, take a bus, and then walk through downtown to get to work. And rarely does anyone make any effort to just chat. Something just seems to keep people from connecting. But one day, this girl waved at me on a bus. So I went up to her and asked "Do you always wave to strange men on the bus?" she said she'd noticed me a couple of times and was new in town (she'd just moved to Seattle from Reno), and that was that. We struck up a conversation and it turned out we had a lot of similar interests, so we started dating. And we're still dating today.*

## BUT PEOPLE WILL REJECT ME!

Will people ignore you, reject you, treat you like you're some kind of dog turd on the bottom of their pointy-toed shoe? You bet. Will married folk instantly activate their "We Shields," designed to ward off all invading singles within a twenty-yard radius? ("Yes, *we've* eaten at this restaurant a few times. *We* think it's really great.") Of course. Will a handful of wishful thinkers misinterpret basic friendliness for some kind of fuck-buddy fishing expedition? Most likely. Will any of this kill you? Absolutely not.

Because for every lustful leer or exaggerated snub, you'll find at least one kindred spirit, someone who's every bit as normal and fun and friendly as you. Naturally, you'll stumble upon a few freaks as well, but so what? Just because you talk to somebody in line at the bank doesn't mean you have to *marry* them. Besides, most of us are pretty adept at spotting the nut jobs. If someone looks sketchy, don't talk to them. If they look normal but turn out to be sketchy, then find a quick excuse to extricate yourself ("Dear God, look at the time! I've got to pick up my wife at chemotherapy!")

As Susan Rabin says in *101 Ways to Flirt* (1997), "The local dog run, the tax accountant's office, or the inside of a noisy train car may not seem like the most romantic places in the world. But any place you meet that special someone becomes a special place to you. Be prepared to flirt with whomever you meet wherever you are, and you're guaranteed to meet interesting men and women everywhere you go."

It doesn't matter if the people you meet become your lover, your friend, or your dinner party story of the decade; the important thing is that instead of closing yourself off, you're open to whatever comes along. Remember, good social skills are something you need in this world whether you're single or not.

Of course, what sometimes comes along is that rare and beautiful thing: the spark. Do not be alarmed. Do not run or faint or collapse in a panic. There will be plenty of time for you to screw things up later on should you two ever decide to get romantically involved. For now, all you need to do is enjoy the moment. Pay attention to what the other person is saying, particularly if they're saying things like "My husband and I are celebrating our fifth wedding anniversary this weekend" or "I saw lots of stabbings back in the big house."

If you like what you hear, tell them you've enjoyed talking to them. At this point, they'll somehow impart to you that either (1) that's all there is to it, (2) they'd like things to continue as well, or (3) they're just as socially inept as you and have no idea how to proceed. Unfortunately, most of these messages are communicated through nonverbal means, which can make it difficult for anyone other than a dolphin or alien to figure out.

That's where risk comes in. If you think the signs warrant it, then pop out your business card. Or mention that you have coffee at the place around the corner every day before work. Or trace your phone number into a pile of spilt sugar. You might even consider doing something really outrageous like asking them if

# Tips for Shy Types

We've all been there. You see someone across a stack of oranges at the grocery store who looks interesting, fun, *exactly your type*. But as soon as you realize you'd like to meet them, your palms begin to sweat and your tongue ties itself into a big lumpy knot. You can't just walk up and start talking to a perfect stranger, your mind whispers. They'll laugh at you, snub you, think you're some kind of creep. Paralyzed by fear, you watch your dream date flit away—again and again and again.

Well, it doesn't have to be like that, says David Wygant, author of *Always Talk to Strangers* (2005). "People need to stop worrying, stop making up dumb excuses, stop the fake fear," he says. "Real fear is when you're on a hiking trail and a mountain lion steps out in front of you. Standing next to a man or woman in the grocery store whom you're attracted to and not being able to talk to them is not fear. That's an excuse."

So how do you nix all that nervousness?

**STOP CRITIQUING YOURSELF.** "Anxiety produces what I call Monkey Chatter," Wygant writes, "voices in your head that discourage you from taking action." People need to quit being so hard on themselves, he says, especially shy types.

**GET OUT OF YOUR COMFORT ZONE.** "I ask my clients, 'Where are you the most comfortable?' And they always say, 'In my home.' So I tell them they need to get out of the house. The best thing to do when you're super-shy is go out tomorrow and just smile at people, at anyone—men, women, kids, dogs, cats. Just do that and see how people respond."

**START WITH SMALL INTERACTIONS.** "Once you're out of the house, randomly say hello to someone in line at the grocery store. Maybe engage in a little small talk and get comfortable with that."

**OBSERVE THOSE AROUND YOU.** "What are they doing? What are they saying? Start picking up clues, figuring out your conversational pointers, then use them. Ask people questions, interview them. 'Is the turkey sandwich good here? Oh really? Have you tried any of their other sandwiches?' Ask a few questions and see how people respond and get comfortable with that."

**PRACTICE, PRACTICE, PRACTICE.** "We all want instant gratification, but it's not going to happen overnight. You have to do the work to get the results."

**ENJOY THE RESULTS.** "No matter how people respond, positive or negative, it's still a response. The first one may be horrible, but the more you do this, the more comfortable you'll get, and the more comfortable you get, the more comfortable other people will be around you. And the next thing you know, you're flirting with someone."

they'd like to get together for a drink sometime. The idea is to give them some way to see you again. Please note: This is not a gender-specific action, unless of course you happen to be living inside a faded rerun of *Father Knows Best*. Passive doesn't play anymore, if it ever really did. As the Romans used to say, *carpe datum*—seize the date. (Not literally, of course.)

"I wish more women were willing to take the first step," says Clayton, a 32-year-old software engineer. "I love it when women ask me out. They instantly get much more attractive."

If they don't respond or if you totally choke, don't fret. Plenty of us have handed our digits out to people only to have them transform into puffs of white smoke. If you misread somebody's signals or they misread yours, it's no big deal. Just move on. At least you've made the effort, which is more than can be said for all those people who bitch and moan about how they never meet anybody and then ignore every opportunity that comes their way.

As Nora Ephron says in *The Cosmo Girl's Guide to the New Etiquette*, "Rejections are awful. But if you spend your life avoiding rejections, you will never meet anyone. And if it helps—any man who rejects you when you open a friendly conversation is probably too fearful and too inhibited or stuffy a person to be any fun, anyway."

## AT WORK

*One of the main reasons for going to work is to get involved with your co-workers . . . What other locale allows you daily, repeated, incessant, perpetual chances to fall in love and get paid for it?*

—E. Jean Carroll, *Mr. Right, Right Now!*, 2004

The problem with finding somebody to date outside of work is that it assumes some of us actually *have* lives outside of work. And many of us don't.

We stumble out of the house at 6 a.m., making up our puffy pillow-lined faces in the car or the bus or some cramped compartment of the El. Even with our triple vente lattes, we're fuzzy-tongued and incoherent—hardly capable of making change, much less intelligent conversation with our fellow commuters. Once we're at work, the maelstrom begins. Meetings, memos, presentations, Power Bars. By the time we finally drag ourselves home (after exercising, doing a bit of grocery shopping, and picking up those new worm pills for the dog), we're pooped. The last thing we want to do is get all spruced up and go out dancing with our friend Grace's cousin from Toledo.

And who would? After working a grueling twelve-hour day, it's a whole lot easier just to zone out in front of *CSI Duluth* and fantasize about that good-looking bike messenger who keeps trotting by your cubicle.

**FUN FACT: Half the people who responded to a survey put out by CareerBuilder.com admitted to dating a co-worker.**

Yes, dating co-workers just makes sense. There's no need to write a winning profile or speed from table to table; all you have to do is throw a stapler and—pow—you've found someone. But not just anyone. Someone you know and feel comfortable with, someone responsible enough to hold down a job, someone you might even have something in common with, even if it is just mutual hatred of the boss.

Having someone to commiserate with is just one of the boons of dating a co-worker. It's also damned convenient. And motivating. Who minds putting in the OT when the person you're putting it in (with) is right there by your side? Raging hormones have inspired more than one brilliant performance. And then there's the possibility of getting lucky at lunch (according to a Lavalife. com survey, 31 percent of us do).

**FUN FACT:** According to a survey by Vault.com, 4 out of 10 workplace relationships result in marriage.

But mixing business and pleasure can be tricky. It can bring our professionalism into question. Turn staff meetings into slow torture. And leave us open to all kinds of career nightmares. Love spats in front of the boss. Naughty emails posted on the intranet. Underpants arriving via interoffice mail. And desire among the cubicles is no picnic for management either. There are productivity issues, concerns over favoritism. Not to mention all those strange noises emanating from the supply closet. And, of course, there's the ugliest specter of all—the dreaded sexual harassment lawsuit. To protect themselves, some companies ask dating co-workers to sign "love contracts," releasing the employer from any responsibility if and when things go awry. Others post "no dating" policies, which only serve to make an office romance—even with that hideous Scott from Accounting—all the more attractive.

What should you keep in mind if you're lusting after forbidden office fruit?

**Big brother.** Make no mistake, he's watching and listening and reading your emails. Don't get caught with your pants down (literally or metaphorically) by indulging in sappy email exchanges, hot phone sex, or coupling in the back of the company van. Remember: Management likes to think it owns you—and your hormones.

**Don't bang the boss.** From arbitrary firings to rumors of favoritism to unofficially becoming the indentured office servant, sex with the boss is usually a lose-lose proposition. If you find that you're in the throes of a fatal boss attraction, consider transferring to another department or reconfiguring things so you're not reporting directly to the person you're sleeping with. Sure, power's attractive, but so are eating and paying the mortgage.

**Your treacherous co-workers.** Yes, they're your lunch buddies, but let's face it, they're also a bunch of wretched gossips. Even your mates can screw things up by implying you're too busy mooning over your new boy-toy down in Engineering to get your projects done on time. Imagine what they might do if they *really* wanted to mess with you. "Gee, I'm sorry, I didn't *mean* to broadcast that email you sent me about banging the new intern in the parking garage, really I didn't."

**Sexual harassment hell.** Sure, you've seen the video. Maybe you've even seen the movie. But you absolutely do not want to see the courtroom drama—with you in the starring role. Well, neither does anyone else out there, especially the guys. If you have your eye on a male co-worker, keep in mind that he is probably going to be *very* hesitant about making any kind of first move. It's not just common sense, it's the law.

**Be discreet.** If (or when) you do find yourself involved on the job, be discreet. And try to remember those all-important boundaries. Just because you're having sex with someone doesn't mean you own them. They have every right to flirt, fight, and have fun with their co-workers without you getting your nose out of joint. Save that for when they get that raise and you don't.

**Breaking up.** Not to be a downer, but 1 of every 10 workers ends up having to leave their job because of an affair gone sour. And some go more sour than others. Spend at least two minutes (say, the amount of time it takes you to get undressed) thinking about the possible aftermath of your affair. Will the person you're crushing on be a good-natured trouper if things don't work out? Or will they ridicule you at staff meetings and sabotage your projects at every opportunity? If it's the latter, then perhaps you should try fixing them up with the new girl who's been eyeballing *your* promotion. Hey, what are co-workers for?

## AT PLAY

*Most desirable social relationships grow out of a common interest. When young people are brought together in large groups, they discover those of like interests and tastes, and they are attracted to each other.*
—ALFRED L. MURRAY, *YOUTH'S COURTSHIP PROBLEMS*, 1940

Are you social? If so, does that mean you're a member of several cultural, political, professional, civic, sports, and/or volunteer groups, formal or otherwise? Or does that mean you go to the bars every Thursday, Friday, and Saturday and do body shots with your buddies 'till two in the morning?

If it's the latter, then you may want to do a bit of reassessment, at least if the sole purpose behind your social agenda is finding "the one." While going to bars can be a hoot—and a great way to hook up if you're looking for some casual fun—it's probably the worst way in the world to make a serious love connection.

### BEYOND THE BAR SCENE

"Most people don't find successful relationships in bar settings," says sociologist Jodi O'Brien. "They find them through their workplace, their church, the places where they volunteer, venues where they have a way of getting to know people. Even if you're a deep, soul-searching person, none of that is going to play out in a bar situation. People only look at what you look like in those venues. It's not necessarily that the people are shallow—it's that the situation is shallow."

In other words, if you're looking for something more substantial than whisker burns on your face come morning, you might want to ask yourself: Isn't it about time I joined a bowling league? A wine tasting group? Some kind of professional society?

"Whenever people work together to accomplish something—whether it's a sport, a church, a book reading group, an arts group, or something educational or political—the jerks are winnowed out very quickly," says dating advice author Tina Tessina. "Go where there are people doing something productive that you're interested in doing and you'll create for yourself a social network, a life purpose, and a place to meet people of character."

You'll also be focused on *something* other than your single status—a professional interest, a recreational goal, or a mutual love of food.

Even the local bridge club can turn into a hotbed of romance, according to Chris, a 42-year-old from Philadelphia.

### Queen of Hearts

*About five years ago, when I was single and in my late 30s, I took up the game of bridge. Unfortunately, it had gone out of style, and the average age of the local club members was somewhere in the late 60s. While I love Harold and Maude as a movie, I never viewed it as a dating primer. As they say in bridge, though, you have to play the cards you're dealt. Not long after I started playing, a brilliant, beautiful 29-year-old woman asked me if I would be her bridge mentor. She was new in town, a rookie at the game. Somehow I managed to find the time to mentor this "queen of hearts," and my bridge partner from the fall of 2002 became my life partner in the fall of 2005.*

## RAISING THE BAR

Of course, telling your friends that you can't join them for martinis because you're heading off to your weekly Scrabble club will get you ostracized faster than a bad case of trench mouth. Yes, even if they are all vapid pits of despair, bars can still be an entertaining way to spend the evening. For some people, anyway. For guys who are on the shy side, they can be the social equivalent of a firing squad.

Perhaps you've been there.

You see her across the room—blonde, petite, a Cosmo nestled in the palm of her hand like a cold pink flower. She looks in your direction and there's a surge of electricity. Within seconds, you're at her side, racking your brain for an opening gambit while one of her friends spins a long rambling story. The story ends, there's a round of laughter, and you touch her elbow. The laughter stops and five women turn as one to glare at you. The petite blonde's eyes become frosty, the electricity disconnected, and you feel yourself growing smaller and smaller. Oops, you've disappeared.

Welcome to the circle of death, that tight clutch of girlfriends who have repelled more advances than Hadrian's Wall.

"Who wants to approach a woman when she's surrounded by five of her most judgmental friends?" asks Michael, age 30. "It's intimidating."

Traveling in packs can make for an eventful evening on the town (just take a gander at that Tweety Bird tattoo on your ass if you need further proof), but it can also kill your chances for meeting a guy, especially one who doesn't have an ego the size of Madagascar.

"A big problem is that women aren't open," says Mason Grigsby, author of *Love at Second Sight*. "They sit around, three or four of them together, and men—no matter what age—are never going to approach a woman sitting in a group. It's like standing up and getting machine-gunned."

Of course, bars aren't just tough for shy guys. They can be a bad experiment in social Darwinism for everyone, particularly those who don't happen to fall into what's known as the Top Twenty.

"Men are visually oriented," says Nathaniel, a 37-year-old bachelor from Seattle. "We have this 80 percent rule. Eighty percent of the men ask out 20 percent of the women."

Yes, despite the sophisticated decor, the upscale appetizers and the chichi cocktails, it's basically a black-leather jungle out there, a hormonal rat race where the most appealing females get to deal with the apes—great and small—and everyone else just gets to watch. As Helen Gurley Brown says in *Sex and the Single Girl* (1962), "If you're not a raving beauty like I'm not, you feel more shy and less beautiful on the prowl in a bar than almost any other place on earth."

## THE PARTY LINE

For those who want the celebratory atmosphere of a bar *without* the survival-of-the-fittest motif, parties are a much better bet. From cozy dinner parties to swanky cocktail hours to New Year's Eve blowouts, you're surrounded by people who have something you'll rarely find in a bar: accountability. Act like a jerk at a nightclub and you'll become a three-minute legend. Do it at a friend's party and you'll be on their shit list for life.

"Parties are the absolute *best* place to meet a potential date," says Andrew, a 35-year-old single from Albuquerque. "Everybody there comes with a reference."

And not only do the people you meet at parties have that all-important social pedigree, they also have one other valuable asset: blabbermouth friends. Just ask Jane, a 35-year-old single from Seattle.

# Know Your Nonverbal Dating Cues

Nonverbal communication can amount to as much as 95 percent of what we "say" to each other, according to David Givens, author of *Love Signals: A Practical Field Guide to the Body Language of Courtship* (2005). While women are usually much better at reading body language than men ("Men are fairly good, but compared to women, they're blockheads," says Givens), all of us can master these basic "stop and go" signs.

### HOW CAN YOU TELL WHEN SOMEONE WANTS TO MEET YOU?

There's something called the "orienting response" that runs through animals—lizards to fish to mammals. Whatever is the most interesting thing in your field of view, you orient toward it. Your body literally turns toward it. It's unconscious and universal. If a person across the room has their upper body aimed directly at you, even if their eyes and head are turned away, it's an invitation to talk or come closer.

### HOW CAN YOU TELL WHEN THAT PERSON DOESN'T WANT YOU TO COME CLOSER?

There's another principle called "cut-off"—it's where the body angles away. If you're across the room or standing fairly close to someone, and they've turned their upper body completely away, that's a sign that they want to be farther away in space. The most extreme version of this is turning your back on someone.

### HOW CAN YOU TELL WHEN SOMEONE YOU'VE
### JUST MET IS ATTRACTED TO YOU?

It's common in courtship to give submissive signals to the
people we like. Some of the best signals for humans involve
the shoulders. You shrug. You lift your shoulders. You flex them
forward. These are coy signals that say "I'm harmless, you may
approach." Another sign is if people start playing with their
hair, either men or women. It relates back to primate grooming.
Eyebrows are also expressive. People who like each other lift
their eyebrows every now and then; it's called the "eyebrow
flash." Another big sign is if someone touches you, or if they
touch themselves. If a woman is sitting down and rubbing her
knee while she's talking to you, it's an implicit invitation for you
to touch her knee. I wouldn't recommend doing that if you've
just met. But it's an "intention motion." In time, they want you
to do that to them.

### HOW CAN YOU TELL IF SOMEONE YOU
### MET IS NOT ATTRACTED?

If they're not giving you any attention, then they're not
interested. If a person swivels around on their bar stool so that
their back is facing you, that's pretty clear. Women understand
these cues a lot more readily than men and usually get the
message right away. But men often won't take a nonverbal no
for an answer; they'll just keep talking. Women may need to
back up nonverbal cues with verbal ones, since men are built
to pursue and keep pursuing until they get a message they can
understand. Many times that's a verbal "stay away"—or a court
order.

### Party of Two

*I met my current boyfriend at a Halloween party thrown by a mutual friend. I was Dorothy Parker; he was a "cereal killer." We chatted for a while and he seemed well-read and articulate, but a little on the shy side. I ended up going out with another guy I'd met at the party (he was dressed as a cow), which my current beau found out when he called the hostess to see if I was available. The cow guy and I didn't work out—no big deal—and I ended up going out on a series of horrid dates over the next eighteen months. Somewhere in there, the mutual friend called my current beau to tell him I was available again and invite him to a small cocktail party. Halfway through the party, everyone left the room where we were talking, and I realized it was a setup. This time, it hit me that this guy was funny, sweet, cute, and, after my forays onto the dating circuit, quite normal. We started going out and have been together ever since.*

While some people dread the banality of polite chitchat, others know that parties can be a relaxed and expedient way to network—and not just for dates, but for jobs, apartments, day-care centers, dentists, and even a few new friends (with benefits or otherwise). Cocktails anyone?

## SETUPS, PICKUPS, MEETUPS

*I've been on so many blind dates, I should get a free dog.*
> —WENDY LIEBMAN, COMEDIENNE

### SETUPS

Oftentimes, even free love can come with a terrible price. "I went on a blind date with Elsie and Dick," an 18-year-old Seattle single named Verna Mae wrote in her diary June 18, 1943.

"The fellow's name was Martin and he was awfully homely!"

Bad setups are so common that none of us even bat an eye when we hear stories like the one about the woman in New Jersey who discovered (at an airport!) that she was still carrying around a butcher knife she'd tucked into her purse before heading out on a blind date three days before.

While we usually don't end up butchering our blind dates, some of us would like to kill the people responsible. Like Andrea, a 32-year-old single from Newark.

### A Date with Mini-Me

*Once, the mother of a close friend called and asked if I wanted to meet her neighbor's son—a lawyer. At first, she wanted all of us to go out to dinner together, but I told her that was way too much pressure. She said she'd figure something out and called back to say, "OK, we're all just going to meet for coffee instead— at his mother's condo." I was too tired to explain, so the next day I met them at the condo. The guy wasn't my type, and his mother was very odd. She was really into miniatures and had a whole room devoted to tiny reproductions of her family home, her old neighborhood, even a bookstore with tiny books on the shelves. It was surreal. I asked her why she was so passionate about miniatures, and she looked me straight in the eye and said, "Because I like to be in total control." Scary!*

So should we avoid setups altogether? Banish any and all who mention the "vivacious" cousin from New Mexico? The "earthy" brother with lots of hair? (Where, we ask, *where* is the hair?) Not at all. Arranged dates are a perfectly viable way of meeting someone—possibly even someone you don't have to wear a disguise with. You just need to communicate a few ground rules to those well-meaning friends and relatives.

For instance, lose the assumptions.

"So many people assume that I *hate* being single," says Andrea, who's endured all manner of bad setups over the years, many of them thrust on her like subpoenas. "It's like they feel that finding a man is the answer to everything."

Assuming life is unbearable for singles has got to be the driving force behind some of the madness that passes for matches. What else could explain the logic of sending a dear friend out on the town with a date who talks of nothing else but their five cats for three straight hours?

If your friends want to find you a match, be clear about your parameters. Give them a few of your interests (hiking, cooking, screwball comedies, *Survivor)* and, more important, a few of your deal breakers (back hair, neediness, fried pork rinds, cats).

Then ask your buddies to slowly back away from the date. Why? Because as anyone can tell you, the worst part about a blind date is not listening to some gap-toothed stranger wax poetic about their last *Star Trek* convention, but the eager look on the face of the person who arranged the whole bloody mess the next time you see them.

"Well?" your co-worker asks after a Friday-night fiasco with her little brother, a gambling addict with a raging case of pinkeye. "Isn't he just perfect? And smart? And cute, just like I told you? I've already invited him to the company picnic this weekend; I knew you'd be too shy to ask him yourself."

Of course, matchmakers aren't the only ones with expectations. We've got a few ourselves. Either we imagine that our blind dates are going to be so hideous that they're doomed from the start. Or we're convinced we're going to meet Butte, Montana's answer to George Clooney. "People create fantasies in their heads about who their dates are before they even meet them," writes Samantha Daniels in *Matchbook: The Diary of a Modern-Day Matchmaker* (2005). "These fantasies make reality very difficult to handle."

If you can trust your amateur matchmaker to find someone genuinely compatible with you (and not just someone they're secretly in love with—another death blow to the blind date), if they can promise to handle the introductions and then do a slow fade (or better yet, arrange a match without even informing the involved parties), and if you can embrace the fact that your blind date is not going to be a science experiment gone bad or resemble anyone from TV (save an audience member from *The Price Is Right*), then you might actually have half a chance.

As long as everyone's mothers stay at home.

## PICKUPS

Pickups can be perfectly innocent—a shared cab that results in dinner and the promise of a brand-new relationship. They can be spontaneous, back-of-the-bar hookups—as fun as they are fleeting. And just as your mother warned, they can also be incredibly reckless, a surefire way to meet the next Ted Bundy.

"You are at a disadvantage when you allow yourself to be picked up on the street or at a bar, for you know absolutely nothing about the man," *How to Get Along with Boys* advises. "You may be exposing yourself to unpleasant advances."

Which may be exactly what you're hoping for.

Annie, 51, of Seattle picked up a guy in the international wing of the San Francisco airport while waiting for her first-ever flight to Europe. "I spotted this really cute guy at the bar and made eye contact with him," she says. "He approached me and we began a conversation that lasted all the way to Germany and even included my initiation into the Mile High Club. His family lived in Heidelberg and he invited me along when they came to pick him up—in a limo. From the airport, we drove to this beautiful castle, where I spent three wonderful days before we went our separate ways."

The traveling pickup is not only prevalent, it can be also be one of the most positive of the pickup genre. There are no expectations, no wasted time, and sometimes there's not even any conversation—you're strictly dealing with the language of lust. But not all pickups read like a fairy tale or a French version of *Penthouse Forum*.

Kelly, a 26-year-old single from Seattle, met a girl at a bar and, instead of indulging in a night of passionate sex, spent the night cleaning up the bathroom after her toilet exploded. Robert, 38, went home with a girl he met at a bar who, 137 phone calls later, turned out to be mentally unstable.

Spontaneity can be fun; sexually transmitted diseases or a stalker, less so. If you meet someone intriguing on the street or in a bar and decide to act on your impulses, just make sure that you're also impulsively safe and sober enough to make a sound judgment call should the situation get wonky.

And don't bother picking out the wedding china on your way home.

## MEETUPS

Wish there was a safer way to stumble onto a date? Well, in Wal-Mart stores in Germany, singles are tying red ribbons onto their carts and strolling the aisles looking for love and low, low prices. In Australia, they're "cereal dating"—wandering through supermarkets with upside-down boxes of breakfast cereal to signal availability. And at Trader Joe's in Seattle, singles have taken to identifying each other by wearing Hawaiian shirts while browsing for frozen lasagna—and love.

You'll find them in cocktail lounges, health clubs, church basements, and online chat rooms. Whether organized by an inspired friend, an entrepreneur, or a group of mountaineers, free meet-ups are becoming a bit of a phenomenon. But they're hardly a *new* phenomenon. As early as 1922, the *New York Times* announced the formation of several "matrimonial clubs" designed to help singles fight loneliness ("For every boy that's lonesome, there's a girl that's lonesome, too," their literature read). Whether they're called dating bureaus, lonely hearts clubs, or social networking circles, singles have always relied on a third party to help them get together.

Why?

"Because it's really hard to meet people," says Samantha MacIntosh, a 33-year-old single who organizes free mixers for friends and friends of friends in Seattle. "Especially good people who are single, available, and in the right head space to be in a relationship."

MacIntosh's mixers, which she's dubbed Dating by Referral, operate on the same principle that fuels her real-estate business—the idea that "good people know good people."

"Basically, I invited a bunch of singles and a few cool couples (who could only come if they brought a single person with them), and then had everyone meet for a happy hour at a local bar," says MacIntosh. "The turnout for the first event was about 40. The second one had closer to 130 guests."

If you live in a singles wasteland (trust me, they exist), you may want to follow MacIntosh's lead and host your own singles happy hour. Or throw a "date swap," asking all of your unattached friends to bring a perfectly usable date (even the occasional ex will do) to introduce around to others. A BYOSSM (Bring Your Own Single Straight Man) party in Miami drew a swanky crowd of one hundred and garnered a write-up in the

*Miami Herald.* "Is this the dating scene of the future?" the writer asked. Yes.

Less calculated than Internet dating, more crowded than set-ups, meetups are a happy medium for those who want to put in only a minimum of actual effort to meet a maximum number of people. Yes, you may have to endure the stigma of attending a Dreaded Singles Event, but guess what—you're single. This also just in—it's not a crime, nor a reason for shame. At least you never have to worry about breaking up with yourself.

Nobody meets a date while sitting at home. So get out there. Sign up on some listserves. Troll the newspapers, the co-op bulletin board, Craigslist. Snoop around and you'll find plenty of meetup options, either through bookstores, churches, volunteer organizations, arts and cultural groups, or through online communities like Friendster, Tribes, MySpace, Yahoo, and, naturally, Meetup.com.

And if you don't find anything going on in your hometown, consider starting something yourself. DIY dating might mean more work, but it also means more control. Instead of hanging out in a bar with a bunch of strangers eyeballing each other like appetizers they may or may not fancy, you'll be hanging out in a bar with a bunch of singles you know or your friends know or the friends of your friends know. However tenuous, there's a connection, and because of that connection, there's a bit less pressure, a bit more context, and perhaps a tad more dignity.

CHAPTER **4**

# LOVE FOR SALE

*"There's gold in them thar singles."*
—HOWARD RYALS, DIRECTOR OF THE FIRST ANNUAL SINGLES EXPO,
*NEW YORK TIMES*, SEPTEMBER 30, 1976

When it comes to finding love, none of us likes the idea of paying for it. Yet, if we're unable to come across it the old-fashioned way, that's exactly what we have to do. And why shouldn't we? Most people recognize how difficult it can be to find a decent date in a society that's more mobile, more neurotic, and more dorky than anything we've seen since the Pilgrims donned those big black hats and sailed off for Massachusetts.

Paying for love may not be our *first* choice, but it's certainly a way we can guarantee ourselves *lots* of choices. But in a world chockablock with matchmakers, dating coaches, social networks, and speed-dating circuits, how do you choose not only which date, but which dating service is right for you? What are the good points, the bad points, and, most important, the worst-case scenarios?

# YOU CAN'T HURRY LOVE—OR CAN YOU?

*Speed dating? That's like Dante's seventh circle of hell.*

—Tony Shalhoub,
*Monk*, 2002

For those few people who haven't heard of speed dating, it's basically the Chinese fire drill of dating. The concept is pretty simple. First you mix and mingle, then you listen to the event organizer explain the rules, then you sit down at a table with a stranger, a bell rings, and you're off.

At most straight events, the women stay in one place all night, while the men go hopping about like hormone-crazed rabbits. After you spend anywhere from three to fifteen minutes talking to your "mini date," the bell rings again and the men change seats. Each date is rated on a scorecard, earning either some version of "Thanks, but no thanks," "Not if you were the last man or woman on earth," or "More, please." If both parties express interest, contact info is swapped and the real games can begin.

And that's that. Most people like it because it's fast, it's efficient, and it's relatively inexpensive, particularly for men, who are often expected to foot the bill for any time spent with a woman. You get lots of face-to-face contact with a score of spiffed-up singles (all of whom are there because they *want* to be there), and you get to do it all in a relatively low-risk environment. There's no commitment, no anxiety about asking for a phone number or a second date, and no need to reject anybody face-to-face.

Which doesn't mean speed dating lacks the basics of any good first date: abject humiliation, instantaneous judgments, and pure unadulterated fear, as Andrew, a 46-year-old single from Chicago, can tell you.

### A Night to Remember

*My first speed dating event was held in a dark, cavernous nightclub. I walked in and spotted two women holding the "speed-dating" brochure who looked like they knew where they were going, so I followed them (I have a touch of night blindness). We walked through the club, then down a hall and through a door, at which point they turned and glared at me, clearly alarmed. We were in the women's bathroom! I made my apologies and eventually found the right room. The speed-dating session started, and at the end of the first three minutes I got up and went to the next table—where I sat in a big puddle of Jack Daniels, courtesy of the guy before me. So for the rest of the evening, in addition to peering at everybody because of my night blindness, I stank of whiskey—every woman's dream!"*

Naturally, there are plenty of success stories out there as well. Go to any speed-dating site—Google the phrase and the URLs will start popping up like baseballs come spring—and you'll find tons of testimonials along with pictures of happy couples mugging wildly behind wedding finery or honeymoon tans. The model has proved so successful, in fact, that businesspeople worldwide have been holding speed-networking events, where professionals scoot from table to table to swap advice, pitch products, and forge new business connections.

Your success rate will depend upon the kind of person you are. If you're outgoing, make a fine first impression, and can deal with quick casual exchanges (and quick casual rejections), then speed dating may be a great way for you to meet your next honey— or your next hookup. If, on the other hand, you're shy or choke under pressure, if blunt rejection (such as someone deciding to "sit out" their session with you) sends you into a tailspin, if the thought of somebody sizing you up with a single glance and a couple of inane questions makes your skin crawl, then speed dating, particularly the three-minute variety, may be far too fast and furious for your personality type.

Naturally, some people like it fast and furious.

"I wouldn't do the seven-minute speed dating. Seven minutes is an eternity—it's biblical," says Susan, a 35-year-old single who has been to several events. "Three minutes is more than enough. You're not going to learn whether the man is a good man inside of three minutes, but it's a start."

What *can* you learn in three minutes? Basically, whether there's a spark.

> **FUN FACT:** Psychologists at the University of Pennsylvania studied data from 10,526 speed daters and discovered that most people make a decision regarding attraction within three seconds of meeting.

Sizing somebody up in three minutes—or three seconds— seem harsh? Last year in England, someone announced the first naked speed-dating event. While sitting around naked in front of fifty judgmental people might be one person's worst nightmare, there are others, as Gail, a 40-year-old single from Asbury Park, New Jersey, can attest.

### Ex Marks the Spot

*A few years ago, a friend invited me to a speed-dating event. Unfortunately, she had to cancel at the last minute so I ended up going by myself. I was pretty uncomfortable going in alone, but when my ex-boyfriend walked in the door, I almost died. He asked if I wanted him to leave, and I told him of course not, that I wouldn't stand in his way of meeting someone. Then I asked him if he wanted me to leave and he said no, he wouldn't expect*

*me to leave either. Needless to say, when it came time for us to
mingle, we were at a loss for words. Luckily, it only lasted a few
minutes.*

Are there other high-speed nightmares? You bet. Michelle
ended up at a table with an angry co-worker who just glared at
her for seven minutes. Helen ran into a guy she'd met at a *previous* speed-dating event who bitched at her the whole time because
she hadn't picked him—"I checked *you*, why didn't you check *me*?"
And poor Elise had to make nice with one mouth breather after
another at her first and last event. Just as with any kind of social
setting, there are people who are obnoxious, people who are funny,
people who are charming, and others who are dull as dirt. And the
good news is every single one of them is available.

"One of the good points about speed dating is that clearly
everybody there is ready to date," says Julie Thompson, who ran
a Seattle speed-dating service for three years. "But some might be
at a different phase in their readiness. Sometimes you'll find people who have just gotten out of something and are simply looking
for that rebound guy or gal. Other times, you'll find people who
are totally desperate—you can practically hear their clock ticking clear across the room. Mostly, though, you'll find people who
are right in the middle."

Even if you do wind up with a ticking time bomb, you have
to deal with them for only a few minutes and then you're on your
way.

"Speed dating is the least painful of all the options," says
Susan, our veteran. "It's a night out on the town, it's kind of fun,
and you're hoarse by the end of it from talking so much. The trick
is to go with a friend and then go out and talk about all the people you met afterward."

Just make sure you go with a friend who has different taste
in dates, advises Thompson.

"I heard about two girls who went to a speed-dating event as friends and they both ended up liking the same guy," she says. "Apparently, they even both started dating the guy, and it eventually got in the way of their friendship. These two best friends ended up not speaking to each other."

# HIRED GUNS

*"Mister Sean Thornton, bachelor, meet Miss Mary Kate Danaher, spinster."*

—THE QUIET MAN, 1952

## MATCHMAKERS

According to some folks, the world's first matchmaker was God, who hooked Adam up with this new girl in town named Eve. His fee at the time: one rib. These days, depending on where you go, it can cost a bit more. According to a February 2005 article in the *New York Times Magazine*, one Manhattan matchmaker's price begins at $20,000. If a match is made—i.e., you get married—then you're generally expected to shell out a marriage bonus, as well. Cars, jewelry, or a big sack of cash seem to be the general idea.

Which, by comparison, makes that rib seem like a bit of a bargain.

Of course, not all matchmakers charge a rib, an arm, and a leg. Seattle's Matchmaker in the Market, Noel McLane, charges $2,000 a pop. And while she might not take you out to swanky parties or refer you to a plastic surgeon the way the higher-end practitioners do, she will give you a full dose of that old-fashioned matchmaker magic.

What exactly does that mean? According to McLane, it means becoming your client's number-one advocate. "I learn as much about my clients as I can," she says. "Then I do careful matching based on very personal knowledge."

While amateur matchmakers like your cousin or your co-worker throw the most unlikely people together willy-nilly, a professional matchmaker earns their keep by conducting a careful search based upon their client's specific criteria, usually gleaned through extensive interviews and questionnaires. If you hate redheads or tax accountants or people who hum, they'll keep that in mind as they go through their databases, spreadsheets, and little black books. And they might just tell you to go jump in the lake for being unrealistically picky. Each matchmaker has their own style and specialty.

McLane's specialty is the personal touch. Other outfits specialize in religious affiliations (or lack thereof). Professional or political interests. Lunch or dinner matches. Matches based on age, ethnic background, or your mail-order bride needs. You'll even find outfits that cater to those ISO money, power, and prestige.

At 4M Multimillionaire Matchmaking Club, owner Christine Stelmack's clients are "men who've made their millions, but not yet met their match." Services are geared toward the "affluent, attractive, highly successful, single professional male between the ages of 25 and 55 who sincerely wishes to meet a deserving woman."

Who are these deserving women? According to Stelmack, they're "single, beautiful, accomplished women in their 20s, 30s, and 40s who can appreciate a man for his character and accomplishments and not just his financial statement." Generally, she charges men $10,000 to $30,000 for her services. Women pay around $250.

So is 4M basically Trophy Wives R Us?

Contrary to appearances (the site runs a continuous loop of toothsome young women in a variety of bewitching poses), Stelmack says no.

"These are career women who have a life of their own but are looking for a good man," she says. "I can't wave a magic wand and say 4M women are gold digger–proof, but I feel really good about my screening techniques."

That all-important screening is a huge reason why many people are tapping matchmakers to handle their soul mate search (that and the fact that we've always liked the idea of somebody doing our dirty work). While online dating is cheaper, it's also much more of a crapshoot—many people feel everyone there either lies like a rug or wears one. Certainly, there are vastly different agendas. Some folks are looking for a serious commitment (the primary reason people go to matchmakers), but others are just looking for meaningless fun. Professional matchmakers do the screening for you, so you don't have to wonder if the man or woman you're meeting for drinks is just after your Monet.

Of course, the $64,000 question is—does it work?

Naturally! say the services. It's Just Lunch, a matchmaking outfit that arranges no-pressure lunch or after-work drink dates, claims their success rate is very high.

"Many of our first dates result in second dates," touts their Web copy. "Every week we're informed of engagements and marriages!"

The bottom line? Just like pierced tongues or thigh-high boots, matchmakers will work for some people and not for others. If you're on a budget, they may be cost prohibitive. If you're too picky ("No, that's not the type of nose I want to date!"), they may not come up with the results you want. And if you're a hideous troll who won't settle for anything less than your very own Britney or Brad, then you're probably SOL (they're matchmakers, not miracle workers). If, however, you're serious, you're sincere, and you're willing to surrender both control and tons of personal information (and you're aware that just because you give somebody a big sack of money to find you a perfect match doesn't mean they can find you a perfect *person*), then a matchmaker might just be the way for you to find your future mate.

## DATING COACHES

If we're out of shape, we hire a personal trainer. If we're looking for a new job, we go to a career counselor. And now, if we're stuck in the dating doldrums, we head to the dating doctor. One of the "newest" hired guns on the block, dating doctors—or dating coaches—came into the mainstream in a big way with the release of *Hitch* in 2005. But they've been around for years, doling out advice on everything from French kissing to fashion to the best way to tell somebody to flake off.

That's because advice is what a dating coach is all about. Advice on how to meet new people, on how to make yourself more attractive, on how to flirt. If you lack social skills, a dating coach can help you build your self-confidence. If you need an online profile that sings, they can do that too. Whether it's getting you reacquainted after being out of the dating loop for a few years, helping you see what you're really looking for in a romantic partner, or letting you know that yes, you do dance a lot like Elaine on *Seinfeld*, a dating coach is like a best friend who doesn't lie. Just like a baseball coach, their job is to improve your game.

"As a dating coach, you teach people strategy," says Chicago's Patti Feinstein, who sells herself as America's Dating Coach. "You tell them what they're doing right and what they're doing wrong. It's like being an internist. You basically sum up what's best for them and then send them off in the right direction."

Some coaches, like David Wygant, spend a lot of time deprogramming clients, undoing years of bad dating advice.

"Many women believe that men are always supposed to make the first move and that it's a man's responsibility to do the courting," he writes in *Always Talk to Strangers*. "Books like

*The Rules* teach women how to play men with regard to this tradition. It's trickery and it's unhealthy. Women must stop buying into this deceptive nonsense on how to draw men to them by playing games."

Other coaches, like Katherin Scott, help their clients define what they want out of their love life.

"You wouldn't go into business without a business plan," says Scott. "Well, you need to create a plan to find true love as well. Some people bristle at the idea, but if you don't know what your requirements are, how do you know if the person in front of you is a match or not?"

Feinstein often works on building her clients' self-confidence.

"People are sometimes afraid that they're not flirt-worthy," she says. "They'll date below their level because they're only able to flirt with people they feel they won't be rejected by. And they freeze up with anyone else. I try to get their confidence up to a point where they're able to flirt on par."

Whatever your dating dilemma, there's a dating coach only too happy to help you fix it—for a fee. And just as with matchmakers, that fee will fluctuate greatly.

Wygant, whose client lists includes millionaires and celebrities (along with regular old joes like you and me), can earn up to $10,000 for a weekend's worth of work. Other coaches will dispense their no-nonsense dating dope for much less. Feinstein charges $250 for an hour-and-a-half consultation, with follow-up sessions running $100 an hour.

Are there downsides to going the dating makeover route? Perhaps. Smooth too many of those rough edges and you may end up creating a completely false version of yourself, a mask that can prove difficult to keep in place ever and anon.

"This is corny, but I think people should be who they really are, who they feel most comfortable being," says Dr. Bella DePaulo, a psychologist at the University of Calfornia at Santa Barbara who studies both singles and deception. "If you start wearing dresses and skirts all the time in order to attract someone, you need to ask yourself—am I prepared to wear all these dresses and skirts for the rest of my life?"

But out-of-control makeovers aren't the only downside to the dating coach trend. According to both Scott and Feinstein, the simple fact that it has become trendy means you have to watch out for the vultures.

"I get really irritated at the lack of credibility and integrity of some people who call themselves coaches," says Scott, who helped put together the International Institute of Coaching in order to provide both certification and licensing for the field. "Thirty years ago, aerobics became very hot and everybody was into it. Half the people weren't even trained, and they were hurting people physically. The same stuff is happening now. People are just hanging up a shingle and saying, 'I'm a dating coach, I can find you a hot date.' Well, there's much more to it."

Feinstein, who's worked in matchmaking and coaching for more than a dozen years, agrees.

"There are a lot of businesses out there exploiting the lonely," she says. "You have to watch who's honest, who's not, and who's really working in your best interest. There are good witches and bad witches."

## SOCIAL DIRECTORS

Along about December 2004, the press started to declare that Internet dating, while not quite dead in the water, had sprung a good-sized leak. It had reached its peak as the hot new dating thing and was starting to be replaced by other bright shiny options. Among the brightest? Social networks, such as

Real Live People Party, an outfit that encourages singles to "shut down your PC and open up to a radical new idea: meeting real live people."

And that's exactly what seems to be happening. All across the country, in city after city, real live people are gathering together at museums, pool halls, golf courses, and dinner tables, courtesy of a cadre of professional social directors helping to facilitate face-to-face encounters, otherwise known as the F2F.

New York has Real Live People Party and the New York Social Network. Chicago has Social Monster and the Chicago Shakers. In Columbus, Ohio, it's Park Place Singles. In Seattle, it's Space City Mixer. While some clubs, like California-based MixerMixer or New York's Social Circles, don't require members to be single (the focus is more on making friends than making dates), others specifically target those looking for love—the implication being that it's a lot more fun and a lot less pressure to search for "the one" while you're playing volleyball, trying out some new wines, or trying to pick somebody's lock.

The latter experience, coined the Lock and Key Encounter, came into vogue about three years ago. The object of the game is for singles to socialize under the guise of solving a simple Freudian puzzle. Men are given keys, women small locks, and then they're thrown together (usually in a bar) and encouraged to "see if they fit together." Aside from the clunky sexual metaphor, the events seem to be fairly popular, as are the organized dining clubs that, much like a good yeast roll, are also on the rise. Although many clubs such as Table for Eight claim *not* to be dating services, they regularly throw dinner parties for an equal number of single men and women (8 Guys Out does the same for single gay guys), matching dining partners by age, lifestyle, and interests. Since the stated purpose is to improve your social network (as opposed to your love life), organizers figure you'll be happy even if all you come away with is a new financial adviser.

Social clubs are basically dining clubs on steroids. They schedule tons of activities—ski trips, gallery walks, cooking classes, baseball games—with some calendars offering up to fifty events a month. For the busy urban professional (the prime demographic), social clubs fill a vital niche; they make all the plans, send out the invites, and provide you with a slew of new friends and activity partners with whom you can pursue that compelling new passion for Cranium or homemade kimchi. For singles who've slowly watched friend after friend disappear down the rabbit hole of love, that's a huge boon.

"I'm single and 32, and all of my friends are either married and having children or they're in some kind of serious relationship," says Nicole, who joined Playdate Seattle. "I have no one to do anything with—even if I just want to go hiking one day, it's a chore to find someone to go with. So I joined this club, not as a dating service or to meet a potential partner, but because they do things every day of the week."

Does that mean every person you meet through one of these social clubs is going to be a fun new friend? Not exactly.

"I went on a hike with one events club, just to check them out," says Louise, a 40-year-old single from Seattle. "And there was this one guy who was extremely annoying. He knew everything about everything; he would come up behind you while you were standing on the edge of a precipice. He even farted in the car, for God's sake. I know it wasn't the club's fault or anything, but I didn't join."

Obviously, you don't have to join a social network or singles club to plum the dark side of the singles pool. Bottom dwellers are everywhere—just ask anyone who's spent any time in line at the DMV. But many clubs do offer screening as a member benefit—which can help a little.

"We can't screen them for social skills—or social diseases—but we can screen them to make sure they're all right," says Elizabeth Tyner of Playdate Seattle. Tyner and her colleagues do extensive interviews with potential clients as well as background checks to flag criminal records, traffic violations, aliases, DUIs, bankruptcies, and divorces (or as she says, "no marrieds, no felons, no creeps").

"We have had guys who want to know what the women are like," she says. "They'll be like 'I want to sleep my way through your organization.' If that's the case, we just say good-bye."

Many clubs invite potential members to check out a few events, free of charge. Why is this a good idea? Because some of these outfits aren't cheap (to be fair, others, like MixerMixer or Space City Mixer, carry no membership fee at all). Most of the time, though, there's a monthly cost of anywhere from $40 to $100—somewhat comparable to either a gym or an online dating membership—or an annual fee, which can run as high as a few thousand dollars.

"I went to this one company and when we first started talking, the joining fee was $4,200," says Julie, a thirtysomething single from Seattle. "But by the time I was ready to walk out, it was $112 a month for the next 18 months. They were like, 'You have to sign up today or you'll never get this deal again.' It was super hard sell. They were even making all these comments like 'Hey, you're not getting any younger.' "

The bottom line? While there *are* a few sharks circling the waters, there are many more legitimate and low-cost clubs where singles can network—professionally, romantically, recreationally, gastronomically, and otherwise. Do your homework (check out sites like OnlinePersonalsWatch.com for more info), ask around, and you're bound to find an organization that suits your needs, your budget, and your temperament. Yes, you'll find the usual mixed bag of singles, but the beauty of the F2F is that you're not dating people who smell like mothballs, you're only bowling next to them. Camaraderie and an extensive cruise directory of events are the best things these organizations have to offer—that and the mechanism for getting you out of the house.

## I SING THE BODY ELECTRIC

*Straight man: Do you believe in computer dating?*
*Groucho Marx: Only if the computers really love each other.*

Ah, the wacky world of online love. The pitter-patter of hearts, the clitter-clatter of the keyboard. Where else—save Hollywood or, say, professional sports—can you find such a rich mix of deception, disappointment, and sheer unadulterated fun? If it weren't for all those testimonials floating around out there (who *doesn't* have a friend or co-worker who found their fiancée on "eBoy"?), Internet dating might have become just another bad fad, the wired equivalent of purse dogs or waterbeds or Sea-Monkeys. Instead, it's become a gigantic moneymaking empire and remains one of the top three ways for singles to find a date. (The other two contenders: meeting someone at work or through friends and social networks, according to a British dating survey.)

> **FUN FACT:** According to an article in the *Miami Herald*, online dating was expected to pull in $500 million by the end of 2005.

For the three people who haven't tried online dating (estimates say 35 million have), it goes something like this. You register with a service, which generally either charges a monthly fee or operates on a chit basis (each chit is good for a certain amount of time or a certain number of messages). Then you post your profile, which consists of a picture or two (tip: use one that doesn't

# Dating Site Roundup

Just like people, Internet dating sites have their own personalities. Some are serious about settling down; others just want to party. To find out the personality of an online dating site, log on to a site like OnlinePersonalsWatch.com. It's filled with reviews, tips, trends, and lists of who's topping the charts in the Internet dating wars (and what sites are being scrutinized for allegedly posting fake profiles to lure potential subscribers). Some current contenders:

**1. YAHOOPERSONALS.COM:** The number-one online dating site. *Everybody's* there, including your mother, your boss, possibly even your neighbor's pet.

**2. MATCH.COM:** More of the same. Tons of hotties, tons of notties.

**3. EHARMONY.COM:** Calls itself the fastest-growing *relationship* site on the Web; definitely not for players or those lacking patience. Known for its extensive questionnaires, eHarmony is all about mate selection and good old-fashioned (heterosexual, thank you very much) marriage.

**4. GAY.COM:** An entertainment and news Web channel with the largest number of gay personals on the Internet.

**5. AMERICANSINGLES.COM:** Part of Spark Networks (which also owns JDate and SilverSingles), AS caters to those seeking relationships, romance, friendship, and the ever-popular "more." Unlike eHarmony, they promise to help you "find a date today!"

**6. TRUE.COM:** "Safety first" is True's motto, and toward that end they do criminal background checks on everybody who surfs their pristine seas, threatening to prosecute any sleazeball who turns out to be married or a convicted felon. And they mean it.

**7. PERFECTMATCH.COM:** Sort of eHarmony Lite, this site offers the Total Compatibility System, a type of Myers-Briggs test for potential couples, plus the advice and expertise of sociologist Dr. Pepper Schwartz. Great for those seeking a honey, not a hookup.

**8. WEBDATE.COM:** Touts itself as the Web's only *free* personals (with events, live video chat rooms, and mobile extras). Good for hip youngsters who have blown their entertainment budget on the latest wireless toys.

Also keep in mind:

**FRIENDSTER.COM:** One of the top social networking sites. Geared toward meeting rather than mating, Friendster offers blogs, profiles, online photo albums, bulletin boards, and a gigantic network through which you can play six degrees of Kevin Bacon. Great for those seeking a hookup (as opposed to a honey).

**SPRING STREET NETWORKS:** Those quirky personals on Salon, Esquire, Nerve, or *The Onion* that start out "In my bedroom, you might find . . ." are all part of this network. SSN exclusively partners with what they term "high-quality media companies," so it's the perfect site for finding those geeky/artsy types.

**BLACKPLANET.COM:** An entertainment and news Web channel with the largest dating site for African Americans.

**AGREATERDATE.COM:** A compendium of online dating and specialized niche sites, divvied up into categories such as "book lovers," "millionaires," "truckers," and "women in jail."

include the disembodied fingers of an ex curled around your arm) and a bit of crucial info about who you are and what it is you're looking for.

Naturally, people are looking for all kinds of things—dinner and a movie, marriage and children, bondage and discipline—and there are Web sites that cater to all of those things and more. Niche sites, in fact, are one of the hottest new things in Internet dating, with specialty sites geared toward pet lovers, bookworms, farmers, vegetarians, rednecks, golfers, seniors, people with hepatitis C, and singles specifically searching for those who are educated, beautiful, active, religious, and/or sexually voracious. Even the most pedestrian sites will tailor their online questionnaires to accommodate specific interests, as Michele, a 38-year-old graphic designer, learned when she went surfing the first time.

### Just a Kid at Heart

*One of the first things I learned about Internet dating was that you have to learn the terminology. I didn't realize that the word "play" was some kind of code word for "open relationship." I thought play meant hanging out, having fun—that it was synonymous with friendship. You know, kayaking, hiking, playing. I'd always thought of myself as a big kid, running around having a good time, so it made sense to me. Then I got an email from a guy who was looking for someone to join him and his girlfriend in a threesome.*

While baffling to many beginners, meeting people through the Internet is actually quite easy, as well as inexpensive, widely accepted, and about as efficient as you can get short of ordering somebody out of the Sears catalog (some might argue it actually *is* ordering somebody out of the Sears catalog). The Internet is also about as democratic as you can get—young, old, gay, straight, fat, thin, red, blue—*everybody's* out there.

"Internet sites dramatically increase the pool of people that you have available to interact with," says Jodi O'Brien, a Seattle University sociologist. "You don't have to join ten volunteer groups or go to ten different bars to meet one or two people. It enables people to connect and see what's available."

But there's an art to it. First, you have to figure out which site will best help you find the type of person you want to meet (dating sites have personalities, just like people). You have to learn the lingo and package yourself appropriately (toward this end, there are a handful of companies that help singles create spiffy profiles and fabulous photos). You have to learn how to quickly and efficiently separate the wheat from the chaff, and from all reports there's a lot of chaff out there—none of whom can spell.

And then you have to be prepared for all kinds of foul human behavior.

## LIAR, LIAR

Big fat liars are probably the biggest complaint of singles who surf. Instead of fessing up about whatever it is we don't like about ourselves (our age, our weight, the fact that we're not so happily married), we simply fail to mention it in order to create a more pleasing virtual self. What happened to Andrew, a 46-year-old single from Chicago, is fairly typical.

### Stretching the Truth

*My entry into the Internet relationship world was marked by a sweet email (and picture) from an attractive, willowy, dark-eyed beauty—with strangely thin feet. We started "chatting" over the Net every day, and after a few weeks I decided to make the three-hour journey to meet my new sweetie for lunch, totally unprepared for the hulking, tattooed behemoth that awaited me. This woman outweighed me by one hundred pounds, was taller than me (I'm 5'11"), and had a deep voice made gravelly by years of smoking and (she confessed) alcohol abuse. After hurrying home (fleeing might be a better word), I studied her picture and realized she had stretched it vertically to make herself appear tall and thin . . . which finally explained those skinny feet!*

Fudged photos and not-so-little white lies are nothing new. According to E. S. Turner, author of *A History of Courting* (1954), during the World War II era, letter writing between soldiers and single women back home was as big as email is now, and lying was just as routine. Sometimes, when pen pals finally did meet, they'd discover all kinds of tidbits that hadn't come up during all that fond correspondence—little things like a brood of children or a long prison record. "Not the least duplicity practiced by unscrupulous pen-pals was to send an old photograph showing the writer as he or she was twenty years earlier," Turner writes, "or even to send somebody else's photograph."

Little has changed in the intervening fifty years. These days, when we're not making up whoppers about our IQ, our annual income, or our breast size, we're coming up with imaginative scenarios that neatly exclude all manner of undesirables like STDs, DUIs, or WIVES. Considering the whole point is to eventually meet up, at which time the truth about that bad comb-over, queen-size caboose, or four children waiting in the car will become painfully obvious, lying seems the height of folly.

So why do it?

"Most of the lies people tell are to make themselves look better or feel better," says psychologist Bella DePaulo. "You want to be a certain type of person or be seen as a certain type of person, and either you don't know how or you're not willing to do the work, so you lie. Lies are like wishes. A person who says he has a full head of hair, wishes he did."

Online lies are also much easier to spin, DePaulo says. You don't have to lie to anyone face-to-face. In fact, you don't even have to do the lying yourself.

"The whole Internet thing makes it very easy to manipulate your words or get someone else to craft a script for you," she says.

Those of us familiar with the movie *Roxanne* know this scenario only too well. A young suitor at a loss for words employs an erudite buddy to help him woo his ladylove. Unfortunately, in the age of the Internet, the bright romantic friend can turn out to be just about anybody, as Renate can tell you.

### Friend or Faux

*I met this guy on the Internet who seemed bright and funny and really into a lot of the things I enjoyed—fine dining, good wines, old movies. His notes were witty and charming, so I decided to meet him. The night of our date, I waltzed into the bar, saw a man waving at me from across the room, and went over to meet him. And the first thing he says is "You shure are purty." I cringed and ordered a glass of red wine, then tried to engage him in a conversation about wine. And he says, in a very slow drawl, that he doesn't drink wine, even though his profile had specifically mentioned it. We decided to get an appetizer, so I chose the hummus plate. And when it arrived, he just stared at it, asking me what that "green stuff" was. After asking him a few questions, I found out my "hot date" lived with his mother, drove an airport shuttle, and despite what his profile claimed, never watched old movies. It finally dawned on me that his mother must be the one who had written all of the messages. I paid my bill and left, and the very next day received a long, intelligent follow-up, which was clearly not from the fellow I'd met at the bar. Needless to say, I had to break things off with mom.*

Lying is a huge concern for almost everyone who goes online, although our fears over what people lie *about* usually depend on who we are. According to Judy McGuire, who writes the syndicated column "Dategirl," it's simple. "Women worry that the guys they meet on the Internet are going to be serial killers. Men only worry that the women are going to be fat."

The best policy? Stick with the awful truth.

"Tricking people isn't going to help you get a date," says Jeff, a single from Florida. "Just be who you are. Everyone stands a much better chance if they just present themselves as is."

## DIGGING FOR DIRT

Some Web sites, like True.com, actually prosecute people for passing themselves off as something they're not—at least the married ones posing as singles. How else can you figure out if you're being snookered by some cyberstranger? Many people use "date-rater" sites like LemonDate.com ("we squeeze the truth out of those profiles!"), where you can post (or peruse) "reviews" of your date's online adventures—good, bad, or ugly. Accountability, in fact, has become a bit of a hot-ticket item; new dating sites like Engage.com let singles post references from friends and family in order to win the confidence of potential coffee dates.

Still don't trust that online suitor? Then simply type "background check" into a search engine, and you'll find plenty of outfits eager to snoop around for a secret spouse or sexual assault rap sheet for as little as $15. Keep in mind, though, not everybody appreciates having their privacy violated.

"If you're reduced to doing background checks on people, you shouldn't be dating," says McGuire. "You should just buy yourself an industrial-sized vibrator and call it a day. Part of dating is risk. I've dated people who have been vouched for by friends, and they turn out to be just as shitty as some stranger. I just don't think it's polite or sporting."

Peter Post of the Emily Post Institute (the final word on polite) concurs. "Investigating someone is an interesting issue," he says. "My initial reaction is that I don't like it."

Googling a date is less invasive and can still tell you a lot, particularly if what pops up is a picture of them at a charity banquet with their husband or wife. But paying attention to cues can be just as instructive. If their profile says they're interested in a relationship that's discreet, they're married—or worse, they're in politics. If they refuse to give you anything other than a cell phone number, or seem to have huge gaping holes where their life is supposed to be ("No, I have no family. No, I don't work anywhere. Where do I live? In my car"), those are big red flags as well.

Sometimes, of course, no matter what you do, you find that you've still connected with Infidelity Central, as Barbara, a 33-year-old single from South Jersey, discovered.

### Worst-Case Scenario

*I posted an ad on Craigslist and a "single" guy responded, emailing me his cell number. I left a message and a few hours later, his wife called back. She politely asked who I was, and I told her the whole story. She was upset but was also nice and smart and said she'd suspected he'd been doing this, but had never been able to confirm it. I asked if she wanted help and she said yes, so we came up with a plan. The guy called me later that day, and*

*I taped his call, casually asking him if he was married, which he denied. We then made a lunch date for the following weekend. That day, his wife got there early so we could meet, then I waited for the guy. When he showed up, he was very sweet; I would never have known what he was up to. We ordered drinks and talked, and then his wife walked up to the table. At first, it didn't register with him; then his eyes opened really wide and his mouth fell open. It was truly a Kodak moment. He tried to tell her he wasn't intending to "do anything," and asked me to confirm this, but I refused. Then I got up to leave and she walked out—with him apologizing the whole way. We all went out to the parking lot, he drove away, then she and I went back in and had lunch.*

Online deception has become such a hot-button issue that even the government has gotten involved. As of this writing, seven states are eyeballing legislation that would force Internet dating sites to either do criminal background checks on members or prominently display warnings that they don't. Concern for the so-called lovelorn is nothing new, though. In a November 1970 *New York Times* article, the New York consumer affairs commissioner warned singles about the dangers of a relatively new phenomenon called computer dating, citing one potential date who walked into a woman's apartment wearing nothing but an overcoat and another who confessed that his "favorite form of recreation was driving to Central Park and stopping at the spot where a brutal murder had occurred."

"Automated dating services which use computers to find the ideal mate capitalize on the insecurity of the lonely," the commissioner claimed. "For too many lonely New Yorkers there is little love and much unhappiness to be found through these services."

## A KID IN A CANDY STORE

These days, though, it would appear there's *too* much love—or maybe it's just too much choice.

> **FUN FACT:** Psychologists at Columbia University found that people who were offered a selection of six different jams were about ten times as likely to buy a jar than those offered a selection of twenty-four different flavors.

Sheena Iyengar, a psychologist at Columbia University, stud ied what she calls the "tyranny of choice" we face each day by conducting experiments that tempted people with varying amounts of chocolate and fancy jams. Her conclusion: More choice can actually be worse than less. In fact, the more choice people had, the more difficulty they had making up their mind. And when there was too much to choose from, people weren't as satisfied with the choices they *did* make.

"The same Godiva chocolate chosen from a set of thirty chocolates is considered to be less delicious than if it is chosen from a set of six," Iyengar says of her results.

How does this apply to Internet dating? Well, go to any site and you'll find hundreds—if not thousands—of beautiful strangers looking for a connection. It's a virtual candy store out there, and many of us are hard pressed *not* to want to nibble on each and every chocolate we see in the window. While some might argue that this obsessive sampling is the very essence of dating, others would call it by its proper name: compulsive shopping. By appealing to our inherently fickle nature, Internet dating transforms people into commodities and, much like any other inanimate object you can order online, upgrading is a snap.

"The problem with online dating is the overload," says Kent, a fortysomething single from Seattle. "The sheer volume of potential

# What Are the Odds of Meeting a Serial Killer Online?

When it comes to Internet dating, the old saw goes, women worry about meeting a serial killer while men worry about meeting someone fat. Well, thanks to our country's high obesity rate (and our stick-figure standards), the odds of a guy coming face to face with his worst fear are pretty darn good. But what are the odds that a woman will end up dating a deadly psychopath?

Ann Rule, who wrote the book on serial killers (a couple dozen of 'em, in fact), says they're actually pretty small.

"I think the chances of meeting a serial killer online are minute," she says. "It's hard to be precise when you're dealing with such an aberrant personality, but the ones I've written about are not trolling online for victims."

According to Rule, approximately 3 percent of all men are garden-variety sociopaths (a tiny percentage of which turn out to be serial killers), which means "they'll con you out of your money or step on your face to get your job, but they won't kill you." Unfortunately, some of these garden-variety creeps are online, but they're everywhere else, too—in the bars, on the job, at the gym. Thankfully, there are warning signs you can watch for. Herewith, Ann Rule's dating safety tips:

**BEWARE OF MEN WHO WON'T REVEAL ANYTHING ABOUT THEIR PAST.** "Watch out for guys who have big gaps in their past, time unaccounted for, men you can't really track back beyond the time you met them, men who won't give you a home phone number or address."

**AVOID JEALOUS, CONTROLLING TYPES.** "At first it's flattering if they're jealous and want all of your time, but it gets worse . . . Pretty soon, they'll want you to quit seeing your friends and family, to quit wearing makeup because you look too pretty for other men. They'll want to know exactly where you are all the time."

**IF THEY LOOK TOO GOOD TO BE TRUE, THEY ARE.** "If a guy is smothering you with love, flowers, jewelry, and proposals like in two weeks' time, move back. Love at first sight doesn't really happen. Attraction certainly happens, but it's not love. Get to know a man over time. Meet his friends, learn his background."

**BE CAREFUL.** "Women need to be careful in anything. I would never meet a man I didn't know anywhere but a public place, like a busy restaurant. I would never give out my home address or too much information about myself. And I would always tell a friend where I was going and even agree to call them once I got there."

**TRUST YOUR GUT.** "As good looking and charming as Ted Bundy was, there was something about him that scared many women away, and they ran. I always say that if you have a gut feeling— a creepy feeling—don't hang around wondering why. Get out of there. Think about it later, but get free. Unfortunately, when you're lonesome and looking for Mr. Right, everything in you will want to fight these suspicions. But you can't afford to."

dates creates 'Datezillas'—people who are always looking to trade up to someone more perfect."

Being the shallow, easily distracted monkeys that we are, we also tend to opt for the thing that glitters.

"When you have this whole big list of people to go out with, you stick with the bright shiny types," says Judy McGuire. "And that can be problematic. The quiet guy who doesn't make the best first impression could be someone completely spectacular, but you screwed things up with him because you became distracted by the hot bike messenger."

So is Internet dating inherently evil? Not exactly. It's just that much like reality TV (or Wonder Bras, for that matter), it can tap into our deceitful, vapid nature—if we let it. "The Internet has made dating infinitely easier for people who aren't into going out to bars or those of us who work in situations not really conducive to meeting anyone but the UPS man," says McGuire. "But at the same time, it encourages a feeling that people are disposable, that anyone can be replaced quite easily."

## PHANTOM LOVERS

But are we disposing of people because of who they actually are—or because they're not who we *think* they are? It's hard to say.

After World War II, an epidemic of GI divorces prompted sociologists to examine the disjointed dynamic between returning soldiers and their wives. One particular phenomenon was so commonplace that it had a name—the pinup blues.

"Overseas, we goggled at our wives' pictures day and night," a soldier explained in a February 3, 1946, article in the *New York Times*. "We stuck them up in our footlockers and argued about whose was most beautiful. Now we get home and our two-by-four pinups suddenly become strange life-sized women. It's when we prefer the pinups that we walk out."

Granted, we don't spend *years* corresponding with someone on the Internet, but we do spend days, weeks, sometimes even months lingering over their emails, gazing at their digital photos. Consciously or not, we build that person up in our minds, making assumptions about who they are and how they feel about us. We write love letters back and forth—as earnest as anything out of the seventeenth century. (If nothing else, the Internet has revived the art of letter-writing.) And when we finally come face-to-face with the real person, we're disillusioned. The girl is twenty pounds heavier, the man is short and bald. Even if their pictures are perfectly accurate, there can be a disconnect between actual person and online profile. They don't seem nearly as warm and loving or funny as their emails—and how could they be? That person doesn't exist, except in our romantic little minds.

Like those soldiers away at war, we've created an ideal out of our Internet pinups. And once we meet them, that ideal is shattered. You might call it the JPEG blues.

Our penchant for creating lovers out of whole cloth might also explain why some of us have become deeply involved with people without *ever* meeting them. Is this wise? Ask Beth, a 47-year-old single from Seattle.

### You've Kind of Got Male

*I've found some really good stuff on Craigslist—a car and a nice office—so I decided to check out their dating, too. I met a few people, endured a horror story or two (like the guy who told me all about his wife's pituitary tumor), and finally started emailing with this one guy who seemed fairly normal. In fact, he seemed great. We emailed every day for three weeks, had these long, involved, funny conversations about everything. But after a while, I finally asked, "Where are we going here?" because he hadn't asked for a picture and he didn't seem all that interested in getting together. We emailed back and forth a little bit more, and then I got a really terse note. "I've decided we're not a good match," he wrote. "Best of luck, good-bye." I'd never even met the guy and I'd been dumped.*

Getting emotionally involved with someone who never comes out from behind the computer screen (either due to agoraphobia or too much algebra homework) is just one of the hazards of online love. Getting cyberstalked or e-dumped is another. Luckily for singles, there are plenty of advice books and "dos and don'ts" to help avoid the most common pitfalls, many of which are posted on the dating sites themselves.

"I have strong opinions about how to use Internet dating services," says Suzanne Schlosberg, who documented her online adventures in *The Curse of the Singles Table: A True Story of 1001 Nights Without Sex* (2004). "It took me years to figure it out. And there's no guarantee that even if you do everything right you'll meet the right person, but if you take certain steps your chances will be better."

Her number-one step? Women need to make the first move.

"If you're waiting for Mr. Right to discover your profile, you might as well be waiting until the Democrats dominate Texas," Schlosberg says. "That's because guys—bless 'em—are lazy. They'll email practically any woman with two eyes, a nose, and a mouth without bothering to ask themselves, 'Hmmm, does she have anything in common with me?'"

When women do the choosing, Schlosberg says, their odds improve.

## UNPLUGGING

So are there other things to keep in mind when it comes to Internet dating? Perhaps just one—figuring out how to get *off* the sites once you've found what you're looking for (which can often just be a break from all that incessant emailing). While signing up can be a snap, extricating yourself can often be harder than finding a profile shot of a guy who's *not* standing by his car. Most sites automatically renew your subscription, so if you miss a deadline you're back in the dating saddle for another three months, six months, a year—whether you want to be there or not.

"I started seeing this woman in September," says Phil, a 35-year-old bachelor from New York. "But it must have been March before I finally was able to get my membership canceled. They kept renewing me. I would have called to complain, but I could never find a phone number."

Sometimes, even when you *have* canceled, you'll still keep receiving tempting emails from the ether, each one filled with photos, links, and tantalizing messages. Shawn, a blue-eyed paramedic from Boston, is interested in meeting you. Debbie, a rock-climbing attorney from Portland, is hoping you'll send her a wink.

You're alone at the keyboard, your lover's sawing logs in the next room. What could it hurt to follow a link here, type an innocent message there? An hour later, your beloved stumbles out to the kitchen for a glass of water and finds you and Shawn in a passionate email exchange—in flagrante detypo.

Before the sun sets, you're suddenly single all over again. Thank goodness, you can still activate your online profile.

## ODDS AND ENDS AND CRAZY TRENDS

What else is going on in the dating world? Well, in China there's a new matchmaking service for celibates. In Russia, love detectives are tracking down those "beautiful, eligible Russian women" to see if they truly exist. In New York, an Egyptian taxi driver is running a matchmaking service out of his cab. And in Boston, a local entrepreneur (and guitarist) has invented what he terms rock 'n' roll speed dating. And then there's . . .

# Internet Dating Rules

Suzanne Schlosberg used Match.com to go on dates with more than fifty guys (she screened hundreds more) during the three-year "dry spell" that inspired her book, *The Curse of the Singles Table*. What did she learn during her great online adventure? Plenty, all of which she's posted on her Web site (www. SuzanneSchlosberg.com). Herewith, the condensed Really Important Rules for Internet Dating:

### SUZANNE'S EIGHT SIMPLE INTERNET DATING RULES FOR WOMEN

**1.** Seek out potential matches rather than waiting for them to email you.

**2.** Don't lie about anything. Ever.

**3.** Don't have more than five email exchanges before either making a date or cutting the guy loose.

**4.** Don't talk on the phone before meeting.

**5.** Meet for coffee first—no dinners!

**6.** Arrive early, buy your own drink, bring a newspaper, and have an exit line.

**7.** Change your search criteria every few weeks.

**8.** Keep your expectations low.

## SUZANNE'S NINE SIMPLE INTERNET DATING RULES FOR MEN

Why are there more rules for men than there are for women? Suzanne says it's because men need more help.

**1.** Don't send generic emails.

**2.** Don't brag.

**3.** Reveal something interesting about yourself in your profile.

**4.** Don't say you're looking for a woman who "likes to laugh" or "likes to have fun." Who doesn't like to laugh? Who hates having fun? You might as well write, "Looking for a woman who breathes air."

**5.** Don't specify what hair color your date should have or—God forbid—a weight limit or breast size.

**6.** Do your homework before a date. Before each meeting, take a few minutes to glance at the profile of the woman you're going to meet and commit a few details to memory.

**7.** Ask questions.

**8.** Don't talk about your other Internet dates while on an Internet date.

**9.** Don't say "I'll call you" if you don't intend to.

## WINGMEN AND WINGWOMEN

Just like your best friend who "accidentally" slops her drink into the lap of the guy who won't lay off, or effortlessly works your Pulitzer nomination into a cocktail conversation, professional wingmen are there to help your game.

How does it work? You and your hired gun (inevitably a good-looking, personable sort) cruise a joint together, and once the target is spotted, your "wing" moves in, providing you with a conversational icebreaker that raises neither eyebrows nor hackles. "Say, I love that ring. Where did you get it?" "Did you say you're in the symphony? My friend Gail here is a flautist." And so on.

On the plus side, a wingperson will provide you with cocktail lounge cred; just by standing next to you, they'll make you seem more attractive and appealing—after all, they're paid to make you look good. On the downside, the whole system is built on deceit. But you can worry about that later—like when your fiancée can't figure out why you don't want to invite the "dear old friend" who introduced you to the wedding.

## CUDDLE PARTIES

Founded by a couple of sex/romance/relationship coaches, a Cuddle Party is a casual gathering of men and women (some old, some young, some married, some single) where the whole point is to snuggle—and nothing else. In other words, you come (um, make that, you *arrive*), you cuddle, you kiss, and then you go away—completely unfulfilled. These events are about affection, not erections (Rule number 7 spells it out pretty clearly: No dry humping!).

Held in private homes, Cuddle Parties come with a small fee (there's no such thing as a free cuddle) and go something like this. You arrive, change into your PJs, join everyone in a Welcome Circle to hear the rules, then dive into a pile of people and canoodle for three hours.

On the plus side, the parties offer a safe venue where singles can enjoy a bit of a snog without having to worry about expectations or consequences or what the hell the expiration date is on that packet of condoms in the underpants drawer. On the downside, it's about as touchy-feely as you can get, so expect the smell of patchouli (if not worse).

## SILENT DATING

The idea is simple. A bunch of singles gather together, either at someone's home or at a bar or club or coffee shop, where they're encouraged to mix, mingle, and converse at length—as long as they don't utter a single sound. Paper and pens are the only means of communicating. Talking, even whispering, is strictly verboten.

On the plus side, silent dating can be a godsend for shy types as well as those with a creative bent. Slightly less contrived than speed dating, silent dating encourages you to communicate however you want—as long as you keep your trap shut. Love sonnets, cartoons, rebuses, even origami will do, which means writers, artists, crafters, cartoonists, or even those proficient in ASL can really shine at these hushed affairs. On the downside, keeping mum for two hours straight may drive some people absolutely batty. Except, of course, for you mimes.

## DARK DATING

An odd hybrid of speed dating, a game of teenage Post Office, and the movie *Predator* (the waiters wear night-vision goggles,

I kid you not), Dinner in the Dark gathers together a dozen singles in a pitch-black dining room where they're served an entire meal—in total darkness. The menu is comprised solely of finger foods (to avoid an unfortunate flatware incident, no doubt); the main entrée, however, is the guests, who are encouraged to flirt like cats in heat.

On the plus side, you get a great meal and a bit of saucy conversation without once having to worry about whether you've got spinach in your front teeth. On the downside, when the lights do come up (usually with dessert), you might find you've dribbled some of that sauciness all over your white silk blouse. And that all that sexy banter has been wasted on your hideous new boss.

## BUT WAIT, THERE'S MORE!

"Blirting" events (flirting via BlackBerry) are becoming the newest way to meet other singles in a bar. Comcast's Dating on Demand lets singles advertise for love via cable TV. "Team dating" has made its debut. And cell phones are getting into the act with mobile technology that can scan the vicinity for any dates that meet your relationship criteria. The next time your phone rings, it could be love on the line.

Truly, there's no shortage of ways to find someone to go out with. Some people even advertise for dates on eBay or telephone poles or billboards or through outrageous "stunt sites" (Find Me a Husband! Will Date for Food!).

And all that effort is eventually going to pay off. You're going to find someone you want to date. Which means you'll have a whole new set of problems on your hands—where's the best place to go on a first date, when do you spill the beans about your third nipple, who pays for the damn movie?

Let's figure that out.

# PART THREE

# YOU AND YOUR DATE

*Carrie: Have you?*

*Mr. Big: Have I what?*

*Carrie: Ever been in love.*

*Mr. Big: Absofuckinglutely.*

—Sex and the City, 1998

# WHY IS DATING SO DIFFICULT?

*I want the fairy tale.*

—JULIA ROBERTS,
*PRETTY WOMAN*, 1990

While hooking up can be a piece of . . . um . . . cake, dating—at least dating with the intention of finding someone you actually care for—can be slightly more problematic. Some people come on like gangbusters and then disappear like quarters down the sofa. Others seem cool and casual and then turn into perpetual need machines. Hearts are crushed, emotions stuffed. And nobody wants to pay for dinner. As Kate, a 26-year-old single from San Francisco puts it, "Dating kind of sucks."

But the burning question is why? With all the dating resources singles have at hand, all the advice, all the sexual freedom, all the choice, all the great lingerie, why should dating suck? What makes dating for love so difficult?

Some people think it's because we've all become a little too mobile. We're without roots and a handy social network of family and friends, so consequently, we're without dates, at least those that click. Other people think our main problem is that we can't commit. Or that we're confused about our proper gender roles. That we're too shallow. Too scared. Too picky. Too in love with ourselves and our careers. That we have too much baggage. Not enough self-esteem. That the guys are all gay, the women all snooty.

Marcella, 36, thinks the problem is passive men. "I would like to go back to men having the balls to ask us out," she says. "To the days when they would walk up and say, 'Hi, I would really like to get to know you' instead of waiting for us to do it."

Jesse, a 27-year-old bachelor, has the same complaint—about women. "I would love for a girl that's interested in me to just walk up and tell me. Why do I have to make all the moves?"

Why should *we* ask? Why don't *they* call? While some of us are content to remain at a cultural stalemate, stubbornly brandishing our respective copies of *The Rules* as dateless Saturday nights whiz by like Japanese bullet trains, others claim there's simply no one out there *good* enough to date—or at least to satisfy our high standards.

"I don't want a drinker, a smoker, or a guy who's bad in bed," says Lisa from San Francisco. "I won't go out with someone unless they have a degree from a four-year accredited university—no technical schools. I don't like earthy guys who wear Birkenstocks. I don't want anyone too thin or too fat. The biggest deal breaker of all is someone who doesn't own a TV. They must have a television; they must have a car. If you can't afford a car, I don't want to meet you."

Noah, 34, of Seattle has simpler needs, sort of. "I want a goddess," he says, "and I just won't settle for less."

Standards are one thing, but huge shopping lists or unrealistic ideals are quite another. How do you tell the difference between exacting standards and an out-of-control sense of entitlement?

"If you want to prioritize the things that are important to you, that's a good idea," says Pepper Schwartz. "But I've seen some ridiculous lists with all kinds of behavioral, physical, trivial qualifications that the person *must* have. If you have a high number of trivial qualifications—eye color, build, exact height, profession, breast size—you can almost guarantee that you'll stay single. In essence, you're daring fate to bring them to you. It's commitment avoidance, but you don't have to own up to it."

Schwartz advises singles to take a good look at their lists and figure out what's negotiable and what's not (hint: a sense of honor is actually more important than a hot body). And keep in mind that "sometimes the imperfections are what make a relationship sing."

But many of us have normal-size lists. And we also have the balls (or the ovaries) to make that first, second, or third move. And our dating life still sucks. Why? Karen, 31, thinks it's because no one follows through. "Why ask for a phone number if you're not intending to use it? It drives me nuts when a guy says he's going to call and then he doesn't." Jean-Pierre, 46, thinks it's because no one trusts anymore. "It's like people—both men and women—are afraid of one another," he says. "We're not all ax murderers."

Clayton, 32, thinks women are too insecure. "Don't be jealous of the time I spend with friends and family. Don't call so much that my co-workers have to turn off the ringer on my phone!" Katie, 31, is convinced that men are simply freaks. "The last few guys I've dated have all pursued me, and then once we've gotten closer, they've just freaked out and gone running," she says. "What's *that* about?"

Is it the men, is it the women, or is it, say, the Brothers Grimm, those two doofuses who popularized the whole Prince Charming scenario in the first place? Because apparently, *somebody's* got to take the blame—either the people we're going out with, or the whole dating system itself, or our own big bad selves: we're not open to love, we're punishing our inner child, we're Peter Pans or Pollyannas or Sleeping Around Beauties. But maybe, just maybe, it's *expectation*—that starry-eyed romantic hope inspired by thousands upon thousands of love sonnets and blockbuster movies and fairy tales, that's the real culprit here.

After all, it's gleamy-eyed expectation that's told us that love is simple and easy and painless. "See how effortless it is," expectation whispers as we watch our hero speed through a revolving door, knock down some woman holding a tray of sandwiches, and immediately fall in love with her. The whole thing takes about five minutes and is as inevitable as a hot plate at a Mexican restaurant. And it can happen to you!

Only it *never* happens to us the way it happens to people in the movies and the sitcoms and all those bad Foreigner ballads. And although as rational beings we understand this, it still sticks in our craw like cinders on silk.

We all want the fairy tale—cement truck drivers and software testers, hat makers and hookers, movie stars and marketing directors. The problem is, we don't all want it at the same time or for the same length of time or with the exact same person who happens to want it with us. And despite the fact that poor Cinderella put in countless years of hard labor (a surefire way to stay fit and develop personality) and actively cultivated relationships with those who could help her in her search for the one (fairy godmothers, enchanted mice and such), we don't want to put in a lick of work to achieve our fairy tale ending. We just want it to happen. One minute we're single and lonely. Poof! The next, we're in a loving relationship.

Why does dating suck? Because dating for keeps *is* hard work. It's hard work to find someone *we* can stand and who can stand *us*, who will be kind to our family and friends and pets and know how to kiss and hold down a job and laugh at our jokes and never ridicule our private tragedies or embarrass us by screaming at the waitstaff. It's hard work to find them and harder work to keep them, especially in a system fraught with easy outs and opposing agendas and enough nutcases to rival Bedlam. Dating sucks because we're complicated, complex, contradictory creatures. Because we *are* insecure freaks who lack manners, refuse to trust, and are so fickle and fucked up that we don't even have the wherewithal to pick up a phone and call somebody that we *like*, for crying out loud.

Why does dating suck? Because much like us, it's both fabulous and flawed—and unfortunately, it's the only damn way we have to fall in love, wonderful love.

# CHAPTER 5

# PREPARING FOR A DATE

*There's something special about a first date . . . A first
date can be the beginning—of anything.*

—ART UNGER, EDITOR
*DATEBOOK'S COMPLETE GUIDE TO DATING*, 1960

People go on all sorts of dates. Some are strictly about sex (the
spontaneous hookup in the parking lot of Home Depot); some
are purely platonic (the movie night with your co-worker); and
still others are the traditional sort, meant to assess whether the
person you're with is a short- or long-term match.

If you're fortunate enough to know your intentions ahead of
time, it can smooth the dating process. You'll then know how to
ask, how to dress, how to behave, or whether you should bother
asking, dressing, or behaving at all. Unfortunately, many of us
aren't exactly sure where our dates are heading, even if we're the
ones initiating them. And even if we *think* we have things completely pegged beforehand, reality can run amok. The parking lot
hookup can turn out to be a lifelong love. The potential husband
can transmogrify into a much more palatable fuck buddy. And that
hot crush we've had for weeks can turn out to be a crashing bore.

"A date is the social equivalent of window shopping," says
Eric, 27. "Would you take a pair of shoes home without trying
them on? Of course not. So why shouldn't it be the same with

someone you're inviting into your life? See what it's like seeing different kinds of people. You might be surprised what the *least* likely candidate has to offer. Be yourself and have fun, and if it doesn't work, then it wasn't meant to work. Besides, one can never have too many friends or acquaintances."

Being flexible and having fun are crucial to your dating success (they won't hurt in the bedroom either). Sure, dating for love is hard work, but that doesn't mean you have to be a pill about it. People have worth—and perhaps even a place in your life—even if they don't turn out to be your lifelong love connection.

"One of my favorite dates ever was a blind date arranged through my fly-fishing club," says Cynthia, 46, of Seattle. "We met for dinner and went through the usual dialogue. And when we were done eating, he pulled out a length of clear fishing leader and says, 'Let's see your knots.' Between fly-fishing, sailing, and climbing, my level of knot competence was fairly high, so I rose gamely to the challenge. It was the start of a great friendship."

But whether a date turns out to be a new fly-fishing partner, a favorite new horror story, or a future spouse, it's all got to start somewhere. And that's with the ask.

## ASKING FOR A DATE

*If he hasn't called by Wednesday night, make other plans for the weekend. Then you must politely decline if he calls Thursday and nonchalantly asks, "Hey hon, what are you doing Saturday night?" Practice the following answer in the nicest voice possible: "Oh, I'm so sorry, but I've already made plans."*

—ELLEN FEIN AND SHERRIE SCHNEIDER,
*THE RULES*, 1995

Traditional dating has always been full of rules, most of them gender-based. Women are supposed to wait around for men to do the asking. Men are supposed to ask three days, five weeks, eighteen months in advance. Men spring for dinner, drinks, theater tickets, and condoms; women respond with cookies, coquetry, and sexual favors. "Let's see, I had the French onion soup, the couscous salad, the crab cakes, and half a bottle of moderately priced wine. That means you get approximately forty-five minutes of making out and a blow job. Oh, just a minute, you did complain about the bill during the entire drive home; let's make that half a blow job."

Thankfully, those silly rules no longer apply. Women pay for dates; men play the coquet. In other words, in this day and age, no matter what your chromosome makeup, you need to know how to ask someone out.

## COMMUNICATE YOUR INTENTIONS CLEARLY

While the check boxes on Internet dating sites make it pretty hard to misread most dating agendas (I'm looking to make out, marry, mess around behind my spouse's back—please check one), being asked out by someone the old-fashioned way can still be puzzling. Is this person asking me out as a friend or as a date?

"It is outrageously confusing out there," says Lisa, a 37-year-old single from Oakland. "It's very hard to distinguish whether you're on a date or just going out with a friend of the opposite sex. There are just no norms anymore. People who seem flirtatious are sometimes just naturally affectionate people."

What can you do to help cut through the confusion? Communicate.

If you're sweet on someone—a little or a lot—give them some clue that it's a "formal date" (this does not mean one of you has to wear a tuxedo). Phrases such as "I'd love it if you'd let me take you out to lunch" or "Would you go out with me Friday night?" should do the trick. Nebulous phrases like "Want to grab a pizza?" can often be misinterpreted as buddy speak, which means your "date" may be free and clear to interpret (or take advantage) as they see fit. If you're specific about your intentions at the ask, you shouldn't wind up taking out some crush for a romantic meal and $250 later find out that they're living with someone and think of you "just as a friend." Take it from Meagan, a twentysomething single from Seattle.

### A Date with Sonny

*I had a huge crush on a man I was working for (he was in a local band and I did the promotions), and I finally asked him to spend a Saturday with me. I'm not sure how I worded the invitation, but I know I was looking forward to a date. That day, we rented a canoe and rowed around a local lake for a few hours, then went to a nice restaurant for dinner. After that, we bought a bottle of wine and took it up to my building's rooftop garden. The sun was setting, the view was awesome. I thought things were going really well so I made a move, and he squirmed away. I told him that I thought I was getting a good vibe, and he was completely shocked. He said he thought of me as a "mom-ish friend." I was dumbfounded, not only that someone could think of me as a mom (I'm in my early 20s) but that I could have had such a romantic date with a guy who thought we were just "hanging out." As it turned out, he had a girlfriend that no one knew about.*

If you like someone for skiing or Sunday brunch or sex—but nothing else—don't mask your lack of feelings in murky dating language. People like to know where they stand, so if it's not a *date* date, don't pretend it is. Use phrases like "Want to see a movie tonight just as a friend thing?" or "I don't do relationships, but I'd certainly like to do you." That will give them the opportunity to respond appropriately—either by telling you they'd be charmed or busting you one in the chops. Feel like you're being strung along by a dubious dater? Then ask them to define their dating agenda—but be prepared for any answer, even the one you don't want to hear.

## GIVE PEOPLE APPROPRIATE NOTICE

Etiquette expert Jodi R. R. Smith, author of *The Girl's Guide to Social Savvy* (2004), advises giving your date at least three days' notice when you ask them out. But not every date is a *date* date. And not everyone makes plans that far in advance—or appreciates those who do. Sometimes, things just happen. Concert tickets land in your lap. Your baseball buddy gets sick.

The amount of advance notice you give a person is usually a pretty good indicator of how much respect, regard, fear, and/or consideration you have for them. So if you call and ask a guy out three days ahead of time, he'll know you are considerate. And a bit anal. And if you ring him up out of the blue at two in the morning to see if you can come over in ten minutes, he'll know you're inconsiderate—and a bit of an A-hole (unless this is the caliber of your relationship).

Try to strike a balance between how you'd like to be treated, how your date would like to be treated (if you don't know, err on the side of thoughtfulness), and the particular circumstances you're dealing with. If you're dating someone spontaneous, a last-minute ask won't be that big a deal (unannounced pop-ins are pushing it, though). If the person's not spontaneous, they'll let you know, no doubt "in the nicest voice possible."

## RELAY CRUCIAL INFORMATION

Some people—for instance, gay men, metrosexuals, and to a lesser extent, women—devote a lot of care and attention to their appearance. So the thought of being inappropriately dressed for a date goes over about as well as a bottle of ketchup at a French restaurant. When you're making the ask, let people know what's on the agenda—dinner, drinks, a baseball game, a trip to Bermuda—so they won't end up looking like a goof wearing sweats to the opera or stiletto heels on a hike. Also, since getting to know each other is the whole point of a first date, plan an activity that includes time for conversation. Brunch, bowling, or a walk along the boardwalk are all fine first dates. A headbanger concert, less so.

Make sure all the logistical information—who, what, where, when, how—is absolutely clear to both parties. Nothing is more detrimental to a first date than crossed wires. Email a reminder a day ahead or swap cell phone numbers, particularly if you don't know each other. That way, if a disconnect does occur, you can quickly sort it out. And for those of you who claim you don't *need* cell phones, the date you assumed was a no-show is currently standing in the rain at the side of the road staring at her flat tire and cursing your technophobic ass.

One more tip for online daters: If you neglected to mention something pertinent in your profile, such as the fact that you have no nose, *now's* the time to come clean. If your true confession is sexually related, however, do hold off until you've established that you're actually going to *have* sex with your date. Nothing is more off-putting than a person you've never met before offering up their genital disorders before you've even shared a cup of coffee. STDs we can live with, gauche assumptions are something else.

## SETTLE THE MONEY QUESTION

With everybody bringing home the bacon, the old gender-specific payment rules have become passé. Even etiquette standbys such as Whoever Asks, Pays! may not apply when it comes to Internet dating. After all, didn't *both* of you mutually ask each *other* out? Why should the person with the penis be responsible for the bill? And what if neither party has a penis? Or both parties? Keep in mind that today's dating world is full of singles of all stripes, each following a different social code, so it makes sense that people will have very strong—and very opposing—views on who gets the privilege of paying the tab. The only true way to find out who has what view is if you communicate this information to each other, preferably before somebody loses an eye.

If it's critical to your psychological and emotional well-being for someone to foot the bill—you, your date, the both of you, the company expense account—relay that up front, during the ask, not during some kind of silent standoff after the check arrives. A simple "How do you want to handle the bill?" or "How about if I buy the drinks and you pay for the movie?" should do the trick. It's simple, straightforward, and it has the added advantage of giving women (or anyone else, for that matter) the opportunity to remove the specter of sexual commerce from the equation.

"My basic rule of thumb is that the person who does the asking does the paying," says Peter Post of the Emily Post Institute. "But many women don't want to be put in a position where they feel as if they owe the guy something as a result of him taking them out to dinner. I tell my daughters to negotiate the paying at the time the ask occurs, not when the bill arrives."

One final note: No matter who offers to pay the tab, both parties should bring enough money—cash or credit—to get through the entire date. Unless, of course, your idea of a romantic evening is being hauled in for vagrancy.

## THE BIG "NO"

What happens when the exact *wrong* person asks you out? Just say no. Thank you, that's very kind, but you have other plans. You're not obligated to give a specific reason for turning them down, unless you truly are going to a business dinner or a baby shower and you want them to know so they'll ask you out again. And you certainly don't need to be rude (unless they become rude and you have no choice).

If you want to soften the blow, you can tell a white lie—you're involved with someone else, you've just been dumped and need a dating time-out, you're gay. But lies can often backfire (for instance, when they spot you making out with someone else in the back of the bar later on). And deceitfulness—giving out a wrong phone number, telling them yes and then standing them up—is just plain foul. If you don't want to go out with the person, the best plan of action is to be honest. Don't go out with them just to be nice (you can't force a spark), and try not to let external forces such as alcohol, exhaustion, or a broken heart cloud your judgment. Otherwise, you'll end up like Lisa, a thirtysomething single from L.A.

### The Dangers of Drunken Dating

*I drunkenly accepted a date invitation from this guy one night. When he pulled up, his car was in shambles (I thought it might break down on the way to the restaurant) and he turned out to be an overweight guy with a mullet, who talked about* South Park *the entire night. Another time, I was wearing my thickest beer goggles and agreed to go out with a man I met at a bar. When I went to the restaurant to meet him the night of our date, I nearly left. He turned out to be an elderly man with a minister wife and two children, both older than me. Realizing your date is a senior citizen when you remember them as a young stud—ouch!*

For those on the receiving end of a rejection, don't automatically assume the person has *no* interest in you whatsoever. Some people truly do have other plans. Others want to test your mettle and see if you're persistent enough to ask again. Still others need a bit of time to sort out the residue of a past affair. Persistence *can* be an attractive quality (when not employed by psycho stalkers); however, if someone is turning you down repeatedly, that ain't good.

"If someone blows you off once or twice, there may be a good reason," says Robert, 37. "But if it happens three times, I never call them back. The three strikes rule is a good indicator that they're either flaky or not interested."

One last tip: If you *are* turned down for a date, don't overreact. Arguing, becoming abusive, or spray-painting unflattering remarks on the person's place of business—"Brianna is a slut!"— are hardly the way to further your case. And dumping on yourself is no answer either. Rejections are just another part of life's grand pageantry. Move on.

CHAPTER 6

# HOW TO GO
# ON A DATE

*When it comes to first dates, there is no such thing as fashionably late. If your date is late and has not called with an extremely good excuse after twenty minutes, it is not ungracious to depart in order to seduce another lady or gentleman at a neighboring bar.*

—Em & Lo,
*Nerve's Guide to Sex Etiquette*, 2004

Many times, behavior will have nothing to do with the outcome of a date. You find someone on the Internet, meet up for coffee, and realize within seconds that they're not your type. It's nothing personal, it's just that you don't happen to like guys with large goiters or girls who blink too much.

Other times, the person's actions on a first date will determine when or if there's a second. Or a third. Or a wedding come June. So no pressure or anything, but first-date behavior can count for a lot. Which doesn't mean that it has to count for everything. Many people realize that performance anxiety is common. "First dates can be nerve-racking experiences," *The Girl's Guide to Social Savvy* advises. "Many people are not themselves because they are so worried about making a good first impression. In general, unless the guy is absolutely horrid, you should go on at least two dates before coming to any conclusions."

What else should you keep in mind?

# GOING OUT ON YOUR DATE

### LOOK YOUR BEST

This seems like a no-brainer except for the number of dating stories out there about guys showing up in stain-encrusted jeans and women arriving with their assets hanging out. Either of those looks is fine if what you're going for is something that shouts "big fat slob" or "skanky whore," and there are certainly times when that's exactly what we choose to project. Projecting that on a first date, however, may not be your true intent. What's the best thing to wear when trying to make a smart first impression? Something that's comfortable, something that's flattering, and something that fits.

"Obviously, the most important date is the first date," says Rebecca Luke, personal image consultant. "You'll want to feel really comfortable because if you feel uncomfortable, then the date may not go well."

Luke suggests wearing "something that you feel good in. And something that fits. If it's a little too big or too small, don't wear it. Sexy but understated is a good first-date look."

It's also important to dress for the event. "One of the number-one things for *everyone* to remember is to dress appropriately," says fashion stylist Susan Levitt. "If it's a cookout on the beach, then you don't want to wear your Milano spike heels. Find out where you're going and what you're going to be doing there, and then dress appropriately. If you're meeting someone for coffee, don't go in like a total schlump and don't go in all overdressed either. Dress appropriately for your age, for the season, and for the venue. And remember, at the end of the day what works in most situations is understated elegance."

Groom yourself carefully beforehand (nose check, ear check, teeth check, fingernail check). Easy on the aftershave and perfume. And don't forget the breath strips. Apparently, the basics are what people care about most.

> **FUN FACT:** In a survey of 5,000 singles conducted by Match.com, 43 percent said fresh breath mattered the *most* before a hot date, 17 percent said they thought stylish clothes were more important, 15 percent thought it was all about a sexy fragrance, 14 percent went for good skin, and 10 percent opted for great hair.

"The biggest issue before you go on a date is that you take a shower, wash your hair, and brush your teeth," says Jane Weaver, health editor at MSNBC.com, which teamed up with *Elle* magazine to query twenty-seven thousand people about dating. "These seem like very obvious things, but the answers from both men and women show us that these are big pet peeves."

Any other grooming tips? Just one. For those of you who carry a lint roller in your car for last minute touch-ups, make sure the thing's not stuck to your ass when you get out.

## MIND YOUR MANNERS

**Be on time.** If your date looks nice, tell them so. If they don't look nice, tell them they look nice anyway. If you're meeting someone for the first time and they're nothing like you expected, don't belabor the point with comments such as "You had so much more hair in your photo" or "Wow, you're really old." Likewise, don't carry on giddily about your date's good looks, beautiful eyes, or fabulous butt. Fawning over anyone other than royalty is bad form.

**Never dump a date.** Even if you know within seconds that they're not your type, don't tell them so and then stomp off like some dissatisfied customer at a used car lot. In fact, *never* flee a date unless the situation is dire, i.e., they turn out to be the stalker you had back in college. Even with "pre-dates" (those ubiquitous Internet coffee dates), try to hang in there for at least twenty or thirty minutes, and then if you do have to escape, come up with some plausible excuse (an appointment, an errand you need to run, a migraine). If you're bad at subterfuge, set up a bad date "rescue ring" with your cell phone company or a friend. Miss Manners might frown, but most people accept the reality that not all Internet dates pan out. The important thing is that you don't rub your date's face in the pan.

**Don't stack activities or dates too tightly.** If you have an event you need to attend immediately following your date, let the person know that there's a time limit (preferably during a pre-date call or email). You may think of your date as an hour's worth of drinks and appetizers, but your date may assume it's a full night on the town. For all you know, they've turned down courtside seats in order to leave the entire evening open for you. If you stack, give your date the option of stacking as well. Also, if you stack back-to-back dates, don't schedule both for the same location (unless you like to live dangerously).

**Give your full attention to your date.** Don't chitchat on your cell or incessantly check your BlackBerry for email messages. Don't eyeball others or be so focused on the party at the next table that your date feels they've developed a better rapport with the waitstaff than with you. Don't ridicule your date about anything—their name, their job, their clothes, their past lives (teasing is fine, as long as both are playing the game). And don't spend the entire date talking about yourself. Make a concerted effort to get to know the person you're with without putting them on the witness stand or dwelling on topics that might be too personal ("Are those boobs real?") or painful to discuss ("So, I heard you just got dumped").

**Be a friend.** If, while out to dinner, you notice that your date has managed to lodge a large chunk of pimento on their front tooth or wandered out of the bathroom with their fly unzipped, try to find some way to tell them so you won't be unduly distracted the rest of the evening. If you're capable of telling them yourself—this takes a certain élan—do so immediately (a friend of mine used to make pre-meal pacts with people to reveal any embarrassing whatnots). If it's too much for you, pretend you're going to the bathroom and ask the waitperson if they can somehow relay this information. A small tip may be required, but then the thing is done. Your date saves face, you save face, and the evening can sail on trouble-free. Please note: If it's pepper in the teeth, it's a lost cause, just ignore it. If something appears to be dangling from their nose, try using a Kleenex a few times yourself. With luck, they'll take the hint.

**Plan an activity.** It doesn't have to be elaborate. It doesn't have to be expensive. It just has to exist so the two of you don't end up staring at each other like two strangers on a German tour bus. If you don't know the person well, don't plan an activity that might make them uncomfortable (i.e., dinner at Hooters, an evening at *The Vagina Monologues*). Do make sure you have plenty of time to talk, but not so much that they feel as if they're part of some '70s encounter group.

**Try to stay reasonably sober.** Part of being well mannered is being cognizant of your behavior, so watch the alcohol intake, particularly on a first date. Aside from losing your inhibitions, you may end up losing your cookies. Just ask John, a 33-year-old single from New York.

### Projectile Dating

*I met a blind date for drinks and she was nice and cute, so we decided to continue the date. We got a bite to eat and split a bottle of wine, then went to a bar afterward for even more drinks. We were just sitting around talking when all of a sudden, she gives me this funny look and then pukes all over the front of my shirt. Fortunately, it was spring so I was able to buy a T-shirt from a street vendor. Unfortunately, I lost a good Gucci shirt and had this girl on my hands who in about five seconds had gone from being totally coherent to not being able to walk. Apparently, she lived in Hoboken, but she was so wasted she couldn't tell me where. So I brought her back to my apartment. We were both a mess, so I gave her a towel and some clothes and encouraged her to clean up in the guest bathroom. Then I went and changed. When I came back in to check on her, I found her hunched over on the toilet, half-naked, passed out, and covered with puke. I rinsed her off in the shower and then put her into the guest bed. About two hours later, I'm in my bed and I hear her come in. She apologized and then crawled into bed with me! Needless to say, nothing happened.*

**Be gracious about money.** If it's not clear who's picking up the tab ahead of time, offer to pay it, then offer to split it, and finally, offer to leave the tip, pick up cocktails next door, pay for the taxi, or somehow show that you're not an absolute churl. If your date refuses to let you pay for anything—not even $2 for the coat check—don't throw a hissy fit. They may think *they're* being gracious, so smile and say thank you, and if you want to date them again, find some means by which they'll allow you to contribute next time (dinner at your place, perhaps?). Likewise, if your date blithely racks up a $100 bar tab and doesn't so much as glance at the check when it arrives, again, haul out your wallet, smile, and pay up. But as with any other kind of off-putting behavior, keep their attitude (and their sense of entitlement) in mind as you ponder future dates.

Finally, never presume anything, particularly when it comes to sex. Keep your clothes on at all times unless you're swimming or someone has specifically asked you to do otherwise. "I'm going to the bathroom" is not sophisticated date speak for "Hey, why don't you get completely naked and slather your body with Mazola?" Sex shouldn't be sprung on people like some kind of wacky party trick—the old exploding snake in a can. Doing so is both disconcerting and confusing, as Jeff, a 45-year-old photographer from Seattle, can attest.

### *Private Dancer*

*I met this woman while I was working on a story. She mentioned that she'd been a dancer in Vegas, but I didn't think much of it until I got to her place for our first date and she asked me if I liked exotic dancing. I said sure, why not, and then she puts in this tape and goes into the other room to "get ready." I'm sitting in the living room and suddenly out pops this leg. And then the rest of her comes out. She's wearing a thong and this skimpy little top and she starts dancing in front of me, doing everything you'd ever expect a stripper to do . . . She even bends over and smacks herself on the ass and says, "The boys always like that." I didn't exactly mind, but I didn't know if I was supposed to go out with her or stuff twenties into her thong. After about ten minutes, she went back and changed her clothes and came out ready for our date. I guess she thought it was the way to a man's heart, but I just figured if she did that for me, she did it for everybody.*

## KEEP YOUR PERSPECTIVE

It's just a date. It's not the first step along a path of lifelong bliss. It's not the worst moment of your entire adult life (with any luck, anyway). It's just an hour or two with someone with really bad sinus problems or an extremely zany laugh. In other words, it's time spent with another wonderfully wacky human being. Embracing the whole Zen of dating can be difficult for those who have a very clear-cut timetable in mind, such as falling in love, getting married, and having two children before the age of 35. They're so intent on their own wants and needs and goals that they forget they're out with another individual with a completely different set of wants and needs and goals.

Your date is not there to fill your shopping list, nor are you there to fill theirs. So don't treat them as if they're a grocery bag full of items that you did or did not order. Learn to appreciate every date—every person, for that matter—for their own talents and gifts, and try to enjoy the time you spend with them, for the sake of the adventure if nothing else.

"Try to look at each first date as two hours of your life that you will never get back," advises "Dategirl" columnist Judy McGuire. "While this may seem negative, if you try to make it a very good two hours, you'll have fun, regardless of whether your date weighs four hundred pounds and is wearing a complete *Star Trek* uniform."

Most of us can endure anything for an hour or two, even grueling ordeals like Thanksgiving dinner with a boyfriend's mentally ill family (I swear to this day the Jell-O salad contained car parts). If you find that your date is not what you expected, just make the most of it. Don't make so much of it that the person misinterprets your joie de vivre as actual interest, but don't sit there like an antisocial lump either. After all, your date may be just as embarrassed to be seen with you as you are to be seen with them.

On the other hand, if your date turns out to be *more* than you expected, if you're having a wonderful time and you're convinced this is absolutely *it*, rein in the hearts and flowers before your thought bubble explodes and gets goo all over everybody.

"If, on a first date, you start imagining your wedding or whether or not your dog and/or mom will like the person, punch yourself in the head as hard as you can," says McGuire. "This is not allowed. I don't care if he is an Orlando Bloom look-alike who cast aside his role on *One Life to Live* for a career in social work. The only thing you're allowed to imagine on a first date is what his 'come face' looks like. Anything more is getting ahead of yourself."

## ENDING THE DATE

*So, how did the date end?*

—Chuck Woolery,
*The Love Connection*, 1995

You've finished your dessert, bowled your last ball, tossed your leftover popcorn into the trash, and closed down the bar. There's nothing left to do now but say good night—or good luck, I hope you find what you're looking for.

Or is there? Negotiating the end of a date can be almost as tricky as asking for one in the first place. And it can be just as telling when it comes to assessing the timbre of your future relationship. Does she like me? Will he put out? Can I dump this loser and get back in time to catch *The Daily Show*? A thousand thoughts lurk behind the nervous glances and soulful stares as the date begins to wind down—curiosity, expectation, sexual tension, a really full bladder. Here are a few more to keep in mind.

## SEEING THE PERSON "HOME"

With the exception of dates where you don't know the person from a hole in the ground (blind dates, Internet dates, etc.), you'll generally want to make some effort to return your date safely "home." Sometimes, home can mean their car or the subway entrance or a taxi. Other times, it can actually mean their front door. Offer to walk or drive them there. Abandoning your date on the sidewalk outside a restaurant or bar in order to grab yourself a bus or taxi will leave them feeling as if they've just been mugged. And it hardly leaves time for thank-yous, which should always happen at the end of any date, even the stinkers.

If your date seems skittish about getting into a car with you or having you get into a car with them, don't take it personally. There could be a number of reasons why they don't want things to carry on. They may have neglected to clean their car for the last eight months. They may have other plans lined up in the neighborhood. For all you know, they may have terrible gas. Whatever the case, it's best not to push, particularly on their stomach. Be respectful of people's boundaries.

Also, if you do end up driving your date home or to their car, make sure you wait until they're safely inside before you leave. Dumping a warm body out of your car and racing off into the night will not produce the type of warm and fuzzy feelings that will get you laid anytime soon, and it may just get you pulled over for suspected homicide.

## THE GOOD-NIGHT KISS

One of the best reasons for seeing a person home (aside from the fact that it's good manners) is that escorting them to their door may give you a chance to indulge in one of the most lovely dating rituals still in existence: the good-night kiss.

Keep in mind, not everyone is comfortable with the good-night kiss. Many people prefer the good night hug, which can be affectionate and noncommittal at the same time. If you receive a goodnight hug, do not attempt to turn it into the good-night dry hump unless your date encourages you to do so. If you receive the goodnight hug accompanied by "the tap" (traditionally three short pats on the back), it's best to wind things down. If your date offers a good-night handshake, don't be insulted or take this as a bad sign. A handshake is still a perfectly respectable way to end a date and may signify nothing more than the fact that your date's jealous ex is hiding in that old Pontiac LeMans across the street. If your date ends with something along the lines of a distant nod or formal bow, it's safe to assume it's not a love match. However, you may have just found yourself a splendid tax attorney or bridge partner.

When going in for a kiss (particularly a first kiss), never pounce on the person as if you're trying to capture a chicken—that can result in chipped teeth, broken eyeglasses, and quite possibly a lawsuit. First ascertain whether your kiss is welcome by telegraphing your intentions with small intimate gestures: the hand on the shoulder, the deep stare (some advise staring at the person's lips), or a subtle statement such as, "Gee, I'd like to kiss you." If your kiss is unwelcome—or unwelcome at that time—your date will let you know. Some dates may be shy or play a bit coy; however, in no way should a sock in the eye or knee to the groin be interpreted as "playing coy."

If your kiss *is* welcome, it's best to start off slowly (sudden and passionate can be incredibly sexy but it's hard to pull off unless you're French). However, don't move so slowly that your date has time to get up and make a cheese sandwich. Em & Lo, authors of *Nerve's Guide to Sex Etiquette*, offer this advice: "When in doubt, follow this order of operations during any given kissing session: 1) Closed mouth, 2) Opened mouth, no tongue, 3) Opened mouth, just the hint of tongue, 4) Full-on tongue probing."

Just as with sex, a good kisser is never a given. And it's almost impossible to determine the quality of a date's kisses without doing your own field research. Unfortunately, as most of us know, it can be a pretty scary field. There are biters. And lickers. And suckers and slobberers and vacuum cleaners and, according to Pam, 46, a few frightening reptiles.

### *Fear Factor*

*I started dating this guy and one day we were laying out on a blanket in my backyard, catching some sun and snuggling. Things started getting more passionate and then he leaned over and basically dove his tongue into my mouth. It wasn't a slow, lingering kiss. It was this quick, wiggling zip-zip of a tongue that made me draw back and go, HUH?! I tried to slow him down, but his snaky little tongue kept zipping in and out between my lips. It was like eating something out of* Fear Factor*! He just didn't get it. I finally had to pretend bees were after me to get him to stop. After that, I hoped things would change—the first kiss often being awkward—but it was always the same. Finally, I just couldn't handle the thought of kissing him anymore and ended the relationship. A year later, a mutual friend knew a gal who was dating him, and apparently her experience was exactly the same. The poor guy was just horrible!*

If you find that you've fallen into the hands (or mouth) of a bad kisser, do your best to hold your own. Gently and respectfully take charge of the situation—ask them to slow down or stop altogether—and demonstrate how it's done. Show, don't tell, is a good rule of tongue . . . er . . . thumb here.

> **FUN FACT:** In a survey conducted by Lavalife.com, 7 percent of singles surveyed said they would tell a date they didn't know how to kiss, 66 percent said they would *teach* them how to kiss, and 25 percent said they would just drop them.

## FIRST-DATE SEX

What if the kissing is going particularly well? So well, in fact, that you realize you'd like to take things to the next level? Fabulous. Before you get naked, you may want to take a moment to welcome a newcomer to the arena. That's right, you and your date are no longer alone—your libido has officially joined the party.

Your libido wants to get laid. That's its job. And it's a damn hard worker, as we all know. Your libido is also crazy powerful, and about as discerning as a pack of fire ants.

Old-school dating arbiters have long warned single women off casual sex by using unflattering references to rumpled merchandise, milked cows, and shabby free-lunch counters. "Why risk having him call you easy—and think of you that way—when he's talking to his buddies in the locker room the next day?" *The Rules* girls ask. Other people warn that cutting *to* the chase will cut *out* the chase, spoiling somebody-or-other's all-important biological imperative.

The bottom line is this: Some people sleep with their dates right away, others don't. Also just in, some folks like vodka martinis while others go for gin—it's all just a matter of style and taste and, most of all, sexual chemistry.

"Why do we all think that sex on a first or even second date is OK?" asks Sonia, a 29-year-old single from Seattle. "No wonder we're bored. There's no seduction, no mystique. I'd like to

## Dos and Don'ts on Your Date

DO

➤ Put thought and effort into your appearance. Floss, brush, shower, shampoo, and shave before your date.

➤ Be on time.

➤ Use silverware correctly, be polite to the waitstaff, and tip well.

➤ Open the door for your date—or anyone else, for that matter—if you happen to reach it first.

➤ Relax and enjoy the moment—even if you don't think it's an immediate love connection.

➤ Ask your date questions, although not in the manner of a prosecuting attorney.

➤ Refrain from sharing the highly personal details—your divorce, vasectomy, abusive childhood, or adenoid surgery—unless you are trying to make a quick getaway.

➤ Accept rejection gracefully.

### DON'T

➤ Stand people up.

➤ Wear scary clothes—red leather pants, a yodeler's cap.

➤ Make fun of people with bad teeth or thick glasses until you've seen your date's teeth and glasses.

➤ Order for your date without asking.

➤ Bring up your STDs or your sexual predilections (no matter how fascinating). Same goes for your thoughts on children, commitment, or marriage.

➤ Confuse one date with another—keep track of your dates, even if it means using an Excel spreadsheet.

➤ Don't call people on your cell phone or IM back and forth with friends instead of talking with your date.

➤ Pick anything on a date, save a good restaurant or fun-filled entertainment.

➤ Forget to bring enough cash or credit to pay for both of you.

single-handedly bring back the art of seduction. Let's make love interesting again!"

Yes, there are a million and one rules why we should avoid first-date sex (He'll never call you again! She'll only think of you as a sex object! Those thighs!), but there are just as many exceptions. On *Sex and the City*, Carrie and Big ended up in bed before they'd even gone out to dinner. But they're hardly the only ones who've started things off with a bang.

> **FUN FACT:** In a survey conducted by *One2One Living* magazine, 63 percent of men and 69 percent of women surveyed had indulged in first-date sex. Furthermore, 79 percent of men and 86 percent of women would consider an LTR with someone they've had sex with on a first date.

"I had one first date where I didn't even leave the house," says Mark, a 23-year-old single from San Diego. "I went to pick her up—I was taking her to a fancy jazz club—and we were both all dressed up and the attraction was just too much. We had great sex all night. I consider it my best date ever."

Rather than worry about abiding by someone else's concept of morality (some people happen to *like* their merchandise a little rumpled and would much rather spend time *in* the bush than beating around it), try to focus on the bigger picture. When and/or if you sleep with someone is a choice based on attraction, timing, standards, and, of course, whether you've shaved your legs lately. Naturally, the other person's thoughts and feelings come into play somewhere in there as well. As does the way they smell. So do it, don't do it, whatever.

> **FUN FACT:** According to the *Elle*/MSNBC.com survey, 41 percent of men found women's unshaved underarms a turnoff, 33 percent

found women's unshaved legs a turnoff, and only 11 percent
specifically preferred a shaved bikini area.

The important thing is that if you do end up sleeping with
someone on a first date (and keep in mind, in today's untradi-
tional dating world, many first dates take place after weeks of
"hanging out"), make sure you're the one making the decision.
Not Ann Landers. Not your sneaky libido. Not the smooth talker
with his or her tongue in your ear. And that you do it safely (condoms always!) and sanely (don't sleep with nutballs, and try to
avoid becoming one yourself).

One final note: If you do indulge in first-date sex, *do* be prepared for any and all consequences, everything from a lovestruck
admirer to a lummox who refuses to acknowledge your existence
come morning.

## A SECOND DATE?

Most of us start sifting and assessing the minute we meet our
dates. We know within seconds of meeting if there's a physical
attraction, and after an hour or two of conversation we generally
know whether we'd like to see them again.

Unfortunately, in today's dating world there are those who
have taken this evaluation process a little too seriously. While
one party is blithely sipping their coffee, the other is silently ticking off items on a mental checklist, humorlessly analyzing every
response. Time is of the essence! An evaluation must be made!
For these folks, dating isn't about casual fun, it's about finding
the best candidate to fill that vacant relationship position.

"How old did you say you were again? Hmmm, 36. I see. I
guess that gives you about three good years before the old biological clock stops ticking. Gee, I'm really torn here. I mean,
you've got a lot of fine qualities—a doctorate in child psychology,
a three-bedroom condo, good teeth, and I must say, a stunning

set of ta-tas—but I'm just a little concerned about those eggs. I'm afraid I'm going to have to pass on that second date. Thanks anyway."

While it's smart to pay attention to the qualities of the person you're out with, don't try to judge their entire worth on the basis of a few short hours. It's impossible, for one thing, and it's incredibly presumptuous, for another. Forget the ticking clock, the pressure from your married friends, the family inheritance—try to live in the dating moment.

"The fine art of developing a friendship seems to be lost," says Terry, a fortysomething single from Seattle. "A couple will go out to a restaurant on a first date and the woman will begin to quiz the guy about whether he wants children or what happened with his divorce. Then she'll make some heavy judgment because his relationship didn't last forever and will cease any further contact. All of this after knowing the person a total of five hours. These are conversations that should happen between good friends after months. They kill the possibility of intimacy when they take place on a first date."

The reason we date is so we can get to know people. And how do you get to know them? By spending time with them, not by hitting the eject button at the first suspect answer.

"One thing I tried to do when I was dating was *not* try and determine if a guy was Mr. Right within three hours of meeting him," says Carly from Jersey City, who recently left the singles scene to marry. "Instead, I'd just spend time with men, trying to understand their heads."

If you'd like to get to know your date better, then by all means ask them out again, either at the end of your date or by contacting them in the days that follow. Let your interest level and nothing else dictate your response time, i.e., don't wait six weeks because you think it makes you look cool. Your date could be engaged by then. Or dead.

If you don't want to see the person again or you're on the fence, then simply thank them for the date and wend your merry way home. Because some people can be positively grim about the dating game, be careful about unintentionally committing to some future plans as you make your good-byes. Avoid using phrases like "See you soon," "Catch you later," or "I'll call you tomorrow," unless you mean it.

## OR NOT . . .

What do you do if it's not a match but your date asks you out again as you're saying good night? Be honest. Thank them for a lovely time and for their invitation, but tell them you don't think the two of you have the right chemistry for a second date. If that seems too harsh, thank them for the lovely time and ask them if you can get back to them the next day (then email or call them with the "'no chemistry'" message—or your favorite pet phrase—as soon as possible). If that's still too tough (or you're too chicken), thank them for the lovely time, tell them you have to pee really bad, and make a beeline for the door.

Yes, it's cowardly, but it will buy you enough time to muster up the courage to give them a straight answer the next time you communicate—which should be sooner rather than later. The important thing is (1) you don't simply ignore the person or their invitation, (2) you don't say anything deliberately hurtful or blatantly insensitive, and (3) you don't end up saying yes just because you don't want to hurt their feelings. That's how people end up in sucky relationships.

"Most guys I know like honesty," says Mike, a 33-year-old single from Los Angeles. "So a word to the wise for women—if you don't want to dance, date, have sex, or whatever, just tell a guy. Cut the baloney, and you and the guy will be better off and happier."

"I would much rather get a clear message than suffer ambiguity," says Cynthia, 46, of Seattle. "I had one fellow who used a red light/green light method at the end of a date. It was great."

What do you do if you feel a huge amount of chemistry with someone, but they neglect to ask for a second date? Well, you can try asking *them* out (contrary to rumor, the earth won't shift off its axis, even if you *are* a girl). You can wait for them to contact you (most of the old-school guidebooks swear by this route, which usually involves a Princess telephone, a simple yet hopeful expression, and cobwebs). Or you can catch a clue and move on.

"If you're interested in someone and they never call back, you've got to read the tea leaves," says Peter Post. "If there's nothing there on that person's part, you're not going to accomplish anything by doggedly pursuing them. Accept the message for exactly what it is. It doesn't mean you're a bad person; it simply means for whatever reason there wasn't a spark. You may have felt there was, but the other person didn't. Don't take it personally. The reality is, you can't make somebody like you."

What, however, do you do if they *do* like you? And *you* like them? What pleasures and pitfalls await those who begin to keep steady company? Let's find out.

# CHAPTER 7

# HOW TO GET ALONG WITH YOUR DATE

*When young people meet only occasionally, it is possible for each to put on his best face. But there are certain characteristics which a person does not ordinarily display before the public that are extremely important in successful mating. Sufficient time should be taken to discover these.*

—WARREN D. BOWMAN,
*HOME BUILDERS OF TOMORROW*, 1938

As difficult as it can be to find someone you click with, maintaining that click can be even tougher. You have to make sure that you and your date are on the same relationship page. You have to deal with issues of intimacy (in a sexual sense as well as an "I wet the bed until I was 17" sense). And you sometimes have to make agonizing choices: Do I care about this person enough to give up my independence, my porn collection, my entire bag of Doritos?

Not that dating is all about sacrifice. There are countless rewards as well—good times, great sex, automatic invites to all those couples-only dinner parties you've been excluded from for months. Having a steady can definitely rock your world. But as anyone who's suffered a bout of seasickness can tell you, being rocked too hard can also make you want to throw up.

Inevitably there are those who would rather sabotage a dating relationship than participate in one. Others find their relationships scuttled by family, friends, or past lovers, who sometimes don't even need to be in the picture to do extensive damage. Even pets have been known to bust up an otherwise promising love match. The challenges are legion.

Will you be able to keep your brand-new relationship afloat? Hard to say, but it certainly helps to be aware of what could be lurking ahead.

---

## GETTING ACQUAINTED

*It is better to know as little as possible of the defects of the person with whom you are to pass your life.*

—JANE AUSTEN,
*PRIDE AND PREJUDICE*, 1813

Ah, that wonderful dating honeymoon period. You've gone out a few times and could swear the person you're seeing is absolutely perfect, and they've reached the same conclusion about you. And why not? You've both been on your very best behavior, used your most stylish manners, and carefully tucked away all of those nasty habits that might otherwise scare the living bejesus out of each other. Of course they like you—they hardly know you!

Me smoke? Oh please, I never touch the filthy things. Thankfully, the restaurant's far too dark for your date to see the yellow stains on your fingertips or the Pall Mall–size bulge jutting out of the side of your tasteful leather bag. When will you tell him that you're a pack-a-day gal? Perhaps tonight. Perhaps after the wedding. Or perhaps you needn't bother, since the way he keeps sucking on his teeth like a crazed rabbit is really starting to get on your nerves.

No matter how hard we try to keep our nasty habits out of sight, eventually they start to creep out into the daylight. And then, for many of us, the dating honeymoon is pretty much over. We're revealed as the toenail biters, bad drivers, or raging alcoholics that we truly are. Just as we assess our first dates to see if there will be a second, we inevitably vet our subsequent dates to see if they'll make it to the next level. The guy who insists on ordering your food every time you go to dinner, the woman who pouts when she doesn't get her way. These may seem like endearing qualities on date one or two, but after a few weeks you start to ask yourself: Do I truly want to be *stuck* with someone that controlling? That manipulative? Are they really worth it?

Of course, not all habits have to be horrific to get you bounced from the dating pool. They just have to be unacceptable to the person you're sharing them with. Just ask Marie, a 29-year-old Seattle single.

### Time's Up

*I was dating this fireman and the first time he brought me home to his apartment, he told me that sometimes people were a little overwhelmed by his collection of antiques. I like antiques so I wasn't worried, but once I got inside I saw it wasn't just a collection—every square inch of his place was plastered with stuff. We're talking old fire extinguishers, signs, gear, ladders, hoses, pictures, toys, articles, and fireboxes. The walls were covered, floor to ceiling, and what there wasn't room for on the walls was stacked up on the floor. But that wasn't all. After the shock of the antiques wore off, I noticed all this ticking. There were clocks everywhere—in the living room, the kitchen, the bedroom, the hall. I thought I was going to go mad. Suddenly, it turned 8 p.m. and the whole apartment just erupted. This was not some little quirk; he'd been holed up in this apartment for fifteen years, never married—except to his antiques!*

# Red Flag Department

An important part of dating is knowing *who* to date—and who to avoid. But considering how charismatic our dates can be (especially during those first few weeks), how do you know who's naughty and who's nice? According to Tina Tessina, psychotherapist and author of *The Unofficial Guide to Dating Again* (2002), it's all a matter of paying attention to the red flags.

## THE CONTROL FREAK

Does your date constantly tell you what to wear? How to drive? Who to hang out with? Can't distinguish between admiration and manipulation? Use this handy guide:

- Intense and persuasive in discussion
- Insistent about making all plans
- Eager to be around you
- Phones frequently
- Showers you with cards, gifts, and flowers
- Displays jealousy
- Displays unpleasant behavior as soon as you've committed

## THE USER/ABUSER

Is your date incredibly charismatic? A little too good to be true? Then they probably are! Red flags include:

- Displays classic signs of the control freak
- Displays anger
- Acts possessive
- Often quite charming and personable
- Displays narcissistic behavior (lacks empathy for your feelings or needs)
- Relationship is one-sided (you give more love, time, and attention and feel unappreciated, drained, and hurt)

## THE DRUNKEN DATE

Does your date's nose appear to glow in the dark? Is their idea of a good time pounding Jägermeisters until 4 a.m.? If so, watch for these telltale signs:

➤ Drinks a lot without showing signs of drunkenness
➤ Displays out-of-control behavior such as rage (at a waitress, another driver, etc.)
➤ Talks about drinking too much
➤ Misses a lot of work
➤ Shows signs of depression or extreme withdrawal

## THE MARRIED DATE

Does your date often call you by someone else's name? Refuse to acknowledge those children at the mall who kept calling them Mommy or Daddy? Holy matrimony! It's a runaway spouse:

➤ Pale spot or indentation on the fourth finger of their left hand
➤ Reluctant to give you a home number or address
➤ Reluctant to let you meet their friends
➤ Reluctant to go "out" anywhere but your place
➤ Inability to spend much time with you

## THE GOOD DATE

These green flags indicate you've found a keeper:

➤ They're cooperative and helpful—if you forget your keys, they'll help you out.
➤ They're self-sufficient; you don't need to take care of them—also, they don't insist on taking care of you.
➤ They're caring and considerate—if you're sick, they'll bring you chicken soup.
➤ They don't try to run your life.
➤ They're interested in forming a partnership, even if it's just a casual partnership.

Opening up to people is risky. We all want to be liked. Yet we know there are certain aspects to our personalities, our belief systems, our backgrounds, and even our physical makeup that may prevent this from happening. And at the same time, we know that unless we reveal something of ourselves to our dates, we'll end up with nothing more than a series of warm friendships, if even that. With every revelation, we come one step closer to being desired—or being dumped.

## TAKE YOUR TIME UNPACKING

Obviously there are many things that can—and should—be shared early on. Vegetarians should let their dates know the score so as to avoid any awkward Outback Steakhouse moments. If you've got kids or pets or some special talent (cooking, canasta, clog dancing), feel free to slap those out there too. Be up front about anything that might prove to be a dating deal breaker—smoking, religious or political affiliations (or lack thereof), the fact that you're seeing multiple people, that you're not actually divorced but separated, that deep down you think you might be gay.

But when it comes to the sensitive gray areas—dysfunctional family histories, past relationship woes, illnesses, gypsy curses—use discretion, especially during the first-blush period. Sure, you're excited to share yourself with your new flame, but opening up the laundry hamper of your life too soon may only send them (or you) screaming into the night. Hold back until a certain level of trust has developed, both on your part and on theirs.

Think of dating as a meal served at a nice restaurant. The waiter doesn't bring your water, wine, bread, salad, appetizer, entrée, dessert, and after-dinner coffee all at the same time.

Then why should you dump everything onto your date's table—or their lap—willy-nilly? Offer up the sweet and savory morsels of your life a little at a time; don't stuff them down your date's throat until they get indigestion, or refuse to give them the tiniest crumb until they have to dine at someone else's table. Intimacy, like a good meal, takes time. And naturally, it doesn't always agree with everyone.

## TALK ABOUT SEX—BUT NOT TOO MUCH

When it comes to sexual intimacy, of course, we don't really have the luxury of keeping completely clam. Otherwise we put ourselves and our partners at risk for disease or even death, which is not only impolite, it's just plain stupid. So when's the best time to start bringing up STDs, IUDs, and other assorted sexual acronyms?

"After it's obvious that you're both attracted to each other but before you sleep together," says "Dategirl" columnist Judy McGuire. "That way you're not wasting your breath telling someone who's not interested in you some deep dark secret. And you're giving your date a chance to make an informed decision. Having sex with someone without telling them you have herpes is really bad form."

But safe sex and birth control methods aren't the only things that need to be discussed before you get naked for the first time. It's also important to bring up any odd physical quirks that might give your bed partner pause. If there's something extra or something missing, be polite and let your date know beforehand. Trust me, they'll notice. Carly, 40, from Jersey City certainly did.

### One Is the Loneliest Number
*I'd been dating this guy for about a month, which was a really long time for me to go without getting down and dirty with a*

*fella, so I was starting to grow suspicious. In the back of my*
*mind, I kept thinking, "Hmm, probably a really small dick and*
*he's nervous." Well, as it turned out, the dick was nice and even on*
*the large size, but underneath, there was only one little brother.*
*He'd made no mention of it whatsoever, so the shock of coming*
*upon it on my own, without any warning, was a real problem.*
*He tried to laugh it off, saying, "I was born that way—like Hit-*
*ler," but that was so not the thing to say to a naked Jewess in*
*her own bed. I told him if he had said something beforehand, it*
*wouldn't have been that big a deal, but he made it into a big deal*
*by ignoring it and then schlepping Hitler into the mix. To be*
*honest, I might have been too freaked out by the middle-hangin'*
*ball anyway. It really wigged me out.*

One thing that *doesn't* need to be discussed ad nauseam is
your long and no doubt illustrious sexual history. Just because
you've shared your love with half the Western Hemisphere (or
just a few key nations) doesn't mean you need to drape your
entire sexual history about your new lover's shoulders like some
kind of carnal quilt.

According to Sandra Gould, author *of Always Say Maybe: A*
*Modern Girl's Guide to Almost Everything but Mostly Men* (1960),
when it comes to sex, the best thing is to be careful, be discreet,
and keep quiet (good advice no matter what your gender): "It's
wise to remember that moral codes change, but not men . . . Keep
this in mind: the less he knows, the happier he will be."

Also, try to remember that the bedroom is not some kind of
sports arena in which everybody's ability is painstakingly ana-
lyzed and critiqued. A little validation is fine ("My favorite part?
Probably when you accidentally kicked the TV set over"), but
don't continually pester your lover about the quality of the performance. It will only annoy them and make you look insecure.

"Don't ask if you're the best," says Clayton, 32. "There is no such thing as the best. We all like different things about different people. It's like trying to compare snowflakes. You just look like an ass when you put someone on the spot that way."

Of course, some people prefer to talk *during* sex, not afterward. And unfortunately, few of them mention their predilection for hot sex talk ahead of time. You usually just figure it out when they start shouting obscenities, as Alicia, a thirtysomething single from Seattle, discovered.

### Look Who's Talking

*My last boyfriend seemed like a dream. Our first date was one of my best ever—we spent the day hiking, flirting endlessly, and talking about everything. Little did I know that talking about everything would become an issue in the bedroom. Our first bedroom rendezvous was like the PG version of* Debbie Does Dallas. *I'd never heard anything like it. Maybe if it hadn't been our first go-round, it would have been a little less shocking. I didn't know whether to be appalled or giggle hysterically. Even months later, this was a difficult adjustment. Every time we had sex, I was afraid of what he'd say (or scream). My inhibitions were at an all-time high and my libido was at an all-time low. So I finally decided to send him on his way.*

If you're the quiet type and you've ended up in bed with a talker (or screamer), you may have no choice but to break things off. But if the person seems like a keeper, you can always try reaching a compromise. Tell them you're into sex play, and use a leather belt (or body part) to muzzle them when they get too loud (kissing works too). You can even try joining in yourself. If all this fails, just come clean (so to speak) and explain the situation. For all you know, the histrionics may be solely for your benefit.

## RESPECT BOUNDARIES (INCLUDING YOUR OWN)

Just as we begin to learn about our date's characteristics (and they ours) during the casual dating period, we also start to learn a bit about their boundaries. Some people are almost too amenable to sharing their personal bubble with a brand-new dating partner. Others would sooner set fire to their hair than share a family dinner, a dresser drawer, or their secret stash of pistachio nuts with someone they consider to be nothing more than a mild acquaintance.

Everybody's boundaries are different, and failing to respect and respond to your date's boundaries can stop a blossoming romance faster than a bad case of crabs. Just ask Michael, 30, of Seattle.

### Out of Bounds

*I met this guy and we ended up going out a few times—coffee, drinks, movies, et cetera—maybe for three weeks or so. We had some playful sex, but we weren't in love or anything. One night we had tentative plans, but I'd had a really rough day at work and wasn't in the mood to go out. When he didn't call, I was relieved. Early evening rolls around and there's a buzz on my door. And I knew it was him. I didn't feel like talking to him or anyone, so I didn't answer. The doorbell rings again and I ignore it again. It stops after a while, so I figured he's gone home. Then all of a sudden, there's a knock on my window. It scared the hell out of me. There's a fence around my building and the courtyard—it's seven feet tall. You can't get into the place unless you break in, and there's this guy banging on my window. I motioned for him to go to the front door and asked him what he was doing, and he started talking about how we were supposed to hang out and how he knew I was home. So I told him, 'Look, we're dating, but we're not a couple,' and told him I felt he had really pushed the friendship envelope. He had no idea what I was talking about, but I felt he had overstepped the bounds.*

Sex can be a huge and seemingly impenetrable boundary for some people.

"I went out with this woman who said she refused to sleep with anyone until the tenth date," says Jon, a 50-year-old photographer from Bellingham. "So I made her this little punch card, like you get for lattes. She was not amused, but we ended up exchanging body fluids after only four dates anyway."

If someone is not ready to share all of their free time with you or introduce you to their circle of friends, their family, or their breasts twenty minutes or even twenty weeks into the relationship, chances are you won't succeed in changing their mind by hounding them relentlessly. Some people are simply slow warmers. It may take months for them to be comfortable enough to introduce you as their boyfriend or girlfriend or allow you to keep a toothbrush at their place—and sometimes this *never* happens.

"Give me my space and I'll give you yours," says Mark, a 23-year-old single from San Diego. "If I want to spend time with you, I'll call. And don't keep mentioning the future. I can't stand it when someone says, 'So whose parents do you want to spend Christmas with this year?' and it's like March. Clinginess is not attractive."

On the other hand, there are those who are not only ready to introduce you to their parents ten minutes into the relationship, they're willing to share their private thoughts and their PIN numbers. It's heady stuff, particularly in the early stages of the dating game. Unfortunately, it's often difficult to tell what's behind it—are they in the throes of love or some kind of monstrous rebound?

Just because someone opens up their life to you, it doesn't mean they've opened up their heart. Conversely, just because someone doesn't want to add your name to their lease after six months, it doesn't mean they don't care about you. We all operate at our own relationship speed. Yes, some people seem to be moving at a crawl, while others tear through emotional boundaries like runners through a finish line. And yes, the longer we go out with someone, the closer we expect to become.

The ultimate boundary buster, though, is not some set time limit, but time plus trust multiplied by true affection—yes, love— an elusive equation that simply may not happen within a casual dating relationship. If it fails to happen within yours and that's what you're hoping for, then by all means speak up. Or move on. Your comfort level is important too. If someone's not crossing your boundaries often enough, and you don't have the patience or the stamina to wait them out, go find someone who will.

---

## GETTING SERIOUS

*Star-dusting, seeing double, going steady! Whatever you call it, it's fun while it lasts.*

—SALLY SIMPSON,
*POPULARITY PLUS*, 1947

Once upon a time, there was only one kind of dating relationship. You went out with someone you liked, took a bit of time to see if like turned into love, and then you either moved on or got married. These days, things are a lot more complex. Relationships have become compartmentalized ("Sure, I like him, but only enough to have sex with, not to go out with"), and love has become as closely guarded as a bad poker hand. Show your cards too soon—or at all—and you lose. Expectations vary; bad behavior abounds. And nothing is a given, particularly whether the person spending so much time in your bed actually *likes* you likes you.

Is it any wonder that we often find ourselves spending more time and energy trying to figure out what our dating relationship means (if anything) than participating in it? Is he husband material or simply a hookup? Is she friend-worthy or more of a fuck buddy? And what happens when we each come up with a different answer?

## WHAT ARE WE?

Dating disparity can be a common problem for the fledgling couple. One person will read an affair as a hookup, pure and simple, while the other has skipped ahead into boyfriend/girlfriend territory. And neither party may be willing to make the other aware of the misinterpretation. Why? Because all that fabulous sex will come to a screeching halt. But if things are starting to get serious—more important, if things are starting to get seriously lopsided—it's imperative that somebody speak up. Otherwise bad shit will start to happen, usually to your vintage record collection.

In other words, if you think your FWB is looking for an LTR and you're not, then get some distance, ASAP. And what if it's the other way around?

"If you start to get all moony about a fuck buddy, you should either tell them about it or you should just quit cold turkey," says "Dategirl" columnist Judy McGuire. "Hanging out with a fuck

# What Kind of Couple Are You?

**HOOKUP:** This is what happens when you drag somebody home from a bar or a baseball game and have your way with them. What that means is entirely up to you: making out, making love, or simply playing mumbletypeg. With a hookup, anything goes—except commitment, of course.

**FUCK BUDDY:** Sex defines this relationship. You don't love each other, you may not even *like* each other—you're just in it for good times. Because of the cavalier nature of this relationship, some people prefer their FB to be someone they wouldn't actually *want* to date, i.e., someone too young, too old, or too unsophisticated to be seen with in public. Some people turn their dates *into* fuck buddies, often without letting that person know. Needless to say, the L-word never comes up—unless you're talking about lubricant.

**FRIENDS WITH BENEFITS:** As the name implies, this is someone you might actually see *outside* the bedroom now and again, which is one reason why the FWB relationship can be one of the most challenging to maintain. On one hand, it's comforting, it's practical, and it's safe. On the other, if you trust them and like them and spend so damn much time together, why the hell *aren't* you dating? A successful FWB arrangement requires both parties to be either ultrasophisticated or incredibly adept at controlling their emotions. Perfect for robots, less so for romantics.

**JUST DATING:** You talk on the phone, email every day, and see each other at least once a week, but so far no one's played the exclusive card. Why? Because you're *just dating*, that blissful limbo stage between casual dating and commitment. Some singles, like serial daters, spend their whole lives "just dating." Others would rather have it be all or nothing at all. While fun and somewhat freeing (you can be "just dating" many people at once), back-to-back JD relationships can also be tiresome (how many times do I have to reveal the dysfunctional relationship with my mother?). At this stage, love is seldom declared except during sex; an admission anything more may result in your being "just dumped."

**BOYFRIEND/GIRLFRIEND:** You hold hands, you watch rented movies in your sweatpants, you may even fart in front of each other. Yes, you are an official couple—and you've got the goofy pet names to prove it. The point at which one reaches the BF/GF stage often has to do with age. At 24, you can end up with a steady by the end of your first date. At 44, it can take a few years to get there. But whether you've known each other ten years or ten minutes, love is definitely in the picture. Due to its serious nature, the BF/GF relationship will often progress first into significant otherness and, finally, marriage. If a breakup does occur, it's usually ugly and may involve picking up your belongings from the middle of a rainy street.

buddy when you're in love with them is just torture. It's like dating a married man."

But what if your relationship is more traditional? You've been dating for months and at this point you're sharing PDAs, you're sharing stock tips, you're even starting to leave personal items at each other's homes. Then one morning, you open "your" drawer and find somebody else's underpants. Granted, you haven't exactly had the let's-not-see-other-people talk (at least not out loud), but when they gave you that drawer you figured it meant things had gotten *serious.*

You figured wrong.

When it comes to a dating relationship (or *any* relationship, some would argue), *never assume anything*—not about exclusivity, not about shared feelings, not even about your rights to the leftover Thai food—unless you've reached some kind of verbal accord with your partner. And even then, smart daters make sure the person's statements jibe with their behavior. For all you know, you could be dating a loopholer, one of those annoying people who carefully follow the letter of the relationship law, instead of the intent. No, they didn't *sleep* with that woman (they stayed awake and humped like rabbits all night). Sure, they're *single* (well, they have been living with someone for six years, but legally they're not *married*).

We all have different agendas (not to mention different moral compasses). And even though sparks are flying and feelings seem genuine and reciprocal, your date's definition of the relationship may not mesh with yours, at least not at this particular point in time. Pay attention to any signals that might indicate you're not on the same relationship page (your gut can be a great guide here, as can your friends, the self-help bookshelf, and even

Dr. Phil). Then you can decide if you're ready to turn the page to join them. Or close the book entirely.

What else should you watch out for during your exciting dating adventure?

## IDENTITY THEFT

Just as people will start to resemble their pets, so daters often begin to assimilate until you can't tell where one stops and the other begins. Unfortunately, some people go too far, becoming pod-like in their ability to mimic the identity (or desires) of their dates. In their rush to be loved, they lose track of themselves completely. Luckily, some of us are able to catch ourselves before we get too carried away, like 38-year-old Pinky from Elmira, New York.

### *If It's Tuesday, You Must Be Pierre*

*I was very shy during my first year of college, but I finally joined the international students union in order to meet new people, and after one open house my date card was full. Each night of the week was some man with a hard-to-pronounce name. There was Prekosh from India and some guy from France who was raised on a horse farm. Then there was Gustav from Germany and a true-blue hillbilly from Appalachia. I started dating all four of these guys at the same time—one every night of the week—but after a while, I noticed that whenever I was with one of them, I'd sort of become this projection of what they wanted. With the guy from France, I walked around with really good posture, like some kind of racehorse. With Prekosh, I kept tilting my head to the side like an Indian dancer. With the German guy, I became incredibly uptight and spit a lot when I talked. And with the guy from Appalachia, I just sat around his apartment drinking moonshine (he had a still). This went on for about a month, until I finally realized they all had to go. I'd become too schizophrenic.*

Hand in hand with losing yourself is stealing your partner's identity. You fell for him because of his artistic sensibility (a painter, whodathunkit?), but now that you've been going out a few months, it seems that he's not so much artistic as apathetic. That garret is far too cramped, not to mention messy (all those dirty brushes!). If he went to work at some kind of arts foundation or maybe even your uncle's print plant, he could make a *much* better salary. Enough to get a bigger place, possibly even a two-bedroom. Sure, he'd have to paint at night, but if it's truly important to him, he'd do it. And if *you're* truly important to him, he'd make the sacrifice, right? As the musical-comedy title goes, *I Love You, You're Perfect, Now Change.*

As exciting as a makeover can be, not everyone appreciates having their entire life reconstructed. Try to remember, you're not starring in some relationship version of *Pimp My Ride*, you're dating. And dating is about celebrating the differences. Once you're married, feel free to stamp them out like scuttling cockroaches.

## SABOTAGE

Getting serious with someone is scary. Which explains why many people find it easier to plant a few relationship stink bombs and then run amid all the smoke and confusion.

"I've had multiple go-rounds with this one woman who can't seem to handle being in a relationship with a healthy person," says Clayton, a 32-year-old single from Seattle. "She freaks out right after saying 'I love you' and starts to sabotage everything.

Things could be really great with her except for this one issue."

Trust, love, dependency—it's horrific stuff, at least for some of us. So it's often easier to push it all away (particularly if we can blame the other guy) and go back to what we know best: our closely guarded, cranky little selves. Some people, of course, would use the dreaded C-word to describe these relationship assassins. But they're usually pretty self-aware.

"I do fear that I may have a bit of the commitment-phobe/player in me," says Daryl, a 28-year-old bachelor. "The five to six-month flings that I usually have all end because I get bored or purposely sabotage the relationship. I guess I'm just not ready to settle down."

Many people are so afraid of commitment they actually manufacture pressure even when it doesn't exist. The mere presence of love and its various manifestations can send them running for the hills. Just ask Julia, a 36-year-old single from Seattle.

### Wedding Bell Blues

*I started going out with this guy I met out on the town one night. We saw each other pretty steadily, and it was just fun—nothing more—which was perfectly fine with me. We dated for a few months and then one day, I took him to a friend's wedding. And at the reception afterward, somebody asked how long we'd been seeing each other. I said, "Oh, five or six months, I guess." And my boyfriend's face absolutely transformed. I swear it turned green and you could almost see the thought bubble appear over his head—the guy was having a complete freak-out. The wedding, the couples, the sudden realization that we'd been involved six whole months—it was all just too much for the poor thing. Not three days later, he broke up with me, said he needed to work some things out.*

Some of us are commitment-phobic. Others are commitment-fauxic. We throw ourselves full-bore into relationships, but only with people who aren't actually available. That way, there's nobody to blame—but them. After all, we're committed, right? "I did that for years," says Carol, 36, of New York. "I got involved with one loser after another. All of whom were completely wrong for me. Then somehow, I finally lucked out and met my husband."

## TESTING, TESTING, TESTING

Two-year-olds do it, software technicians do it, and so do people in relationships. Why? Because we're human—which means we're basically hideous, but we can thumb-wrestle really well. Bad behavior is often a kind of test that people throw at each other to see how far they can push things in a relationship. You might call it the doormat test. Try not to fail it. Nice people often do, because they don't understand the whole nature of testing. They wouldn't dream of treating someone they care about shabbily, so when their boyfriend or girlfriend is manipulative or cruel or treats them like dirt, they reach into their backpack for an excuse. He's tired. She's forgetful. I'm probably just reading too much into it. The dog ate my relationship.

Testing goes on all the time—over big things and small. People will push at the boundaries, scribble in the margins, question authority, and cheat as often as they feel they can get away with it. If somebody throws some kind of relationship pop quiz at you, make sure you get an A, like Phoebe, this 27-year-old single from San Bernardino.

### *Walking Papers*

*I was in this long relationship with a guy that basically went sour because he wouldn't go on walks with me. As a writer I found that my best ideas came to me while I was tooling around the neighborhood. But my boyfriend hated it. In fact, he even started suggesting that there was something wrong with my*

*brain chemistry because I "needed" to take these walks. It became*
*this huge power struggle, and I started to feel like a dog, begging*
*him to put my leash on every night. I would finally just go out*
*alone, patrolling the suburbs feeling very much out of sync with*
*him. We eventually broke up over it. As stupid as it sounds now,*
*I swear I'll never date another guy who doesn't like walking.*

But what if you've somehow managed to negotiate the tests
and the traps? You're spending tons of time together, you're buying bulk condoms at Costco. People have muttered "get a room"
behind your back at the movies and your friends have threatened
to put your face on the side of a milk carton. Is this it? Are you
falling in love? Could be.

According to *So You Think It's Love: Dating, Necking, Petting*
*and Going Steady* (1950), true love has to withstand the test of
time, the test of separation, and the test of companionship (I'd
recommend a test for STDs and possibly an SAT as well). Dr.
Judy Kuriansky, author of *The Complete Idiot's Guide to Dating*
(1996), says things are getting serious when you start canceling
dates with your single buddies, find yourself thinking of ways to
please your lover, and start using "we" instead of "I" or "you."
But there a few other surefire signs that love is in the air.

## BLASTS FROM THE PAST

One of the best indicators that you're starting to fall for someone
is that your ex magically appears on the scene. Sometimes they
show up bearing a huge bouquet of flowers and a passel full of
promises. Other times they call to say they're getting married or
they just wanted to hear your voice. No one can explain why this

happens (private detectives, hidden microphones, pheromone-sniffing dogs?), but it's more common than bladder infections at Niagara Falls.

Although discombobulating, the reappearance of an ex (yours, theirs, sometimes one of each) can prove useful. Why? Because they act as a whetstone upon which your feelings will either grow sharper or be worn down to nothing. Just ask Jeff, a 36-year-old single from Duluth.

### *Timber!*

*I met this guy on the Internet and he turned out to be funny, smart, and have similar interests to mine—very solid timber. Our first date lasted about six hours—we talked nonstop—and after that we started seeing each other pretty regularly. And it was great until the guy's ex-boyfriend, who was somewhat unstable, entered the picture. My guy hadn't mentioned him during our first couple of dates. But after the topic came up, he came up in every conversation. The real kicker came one night when the ex called him from the mental ward of the local hospital. Turns out he'd tried to kill himself. Again. Naturally, my guy rushed to his side and the details of that filled up our next date, which was also our last date. Looking back, I certainly don't hold it against him for being compassionate or concerned. But the real lesson I learned was to never try to compete for the attention of a guy with a suicidal ex.*

## FREAK-OUTS

Another surefire sign that something's afoot is that suddenly everybody around you starts having a nut-out. Your best buddy decides your new girlfriend is a bitch and won't have anything further to do with her or you. Your grandmother threatens to cut you out of the will if you so much as think about marrying that mechanic. And your cat starts pooping on your favorite chair whenever your new sweetie spends the night. Has the world gone insane? No, the relationship gods are simply testing your love.

Sometimes your new squeeze is the one who suddenly starts acting like a weirdo. They don't call when they say they will, they ignore you when you're out with their friends, they pick a fight so they won't have to go to your folks' place for Easter dinner. Or maybe, just maybe, it's you. Who says you can't flirt with the hottie sitting next to you at the bar? After all, it's not like so-and-so *owns* you, it's not like you're *married*. At least not yet.

A case of the freak-outs is a sure sign that *somebody's* thinking about love and commitment, though, either above or below the surface. Because as much as love is grand, it's also pretty terrifying, which explains why everybody around you is suddenly on relationship red alert.

Couples who are meant to be will usually be able to navigate their way through the freak-out period just fine; others may blow out like a bald tire. If your date's bad behavior continues past this sussing-out period, it generally just means you've accidentally become involved with a jerk. Cut your losses and move on.

## LOVE SICKNESS

What's the most accurate bellwether of all? You start to act like you're mentally ill, of course.

You walk around in the rain with a goofy grin on your face. You recite Shakespeare sonnets to little old ladies on the bus. You become obsessed, you become feverish, you stand on the sidewalk at four in the morning and scream your lover's name at a dark shaded window ("Stella!"). You forget to eat, you forget to shower, you even forget that the world is not entirely enchanted by the sight of you and your beloved dry-humping on the hood of your Buick Skylark.

FUN FACT: In a survey conducted by Lavalife.com, 16 percent of singles surveyed said they had had sex in a movie theater, 31 percent said they'd had sex at the office, 13 percent said they'd had sex in an elevator, and 30 percent said they'd had sex in some other public forum.

"Love sickness has very similar consequences to mental illness," writes Dr. Frank Tallis in *Love Sick: Love as a Mental Illness* (2004). "When we fall in love, we immediately begin to stumble across the boundary lines that psychiatrists use to cordon off abnormality."

According to a May 2005 article in the *New York Times*, a team of scientists have even produced brain scans indicating that white-hot love essentially sears the brain, producing much the same effect as uncontrollable urges like hunger or thirst. "In an analysis of the images appearing today in *The Journal of Neurophysiology*," reporter Benedict Carey writes, "researchers in New York and New Jersey argue that romantic love is a biological urge distinct from sexual arousal. It is closer in its neural profile to drives like hunger, thirst, or drug-craving, the researchers assert, than to emotional states like excitement or affection."

In other words, now there's official scientific proof that people in love really are crazy as loons. What else would explain that whole "you're Schmoopie, no *you're* Schmoopie" business?

Have you magically lost five pounds overnight? Found yourself humming Frank Sinatra tunes while scrubbing grout in the shower? Developed a passionate new interest in kayaking? Kabbalah? The Dallas Cowboys? Do your friends groan whenever you mention your lover's name? Are you deliriously happy? Morosely depressed? Incredibly tired, yet thrumming with energy the minute you hear your beloved's voice?

If so, chances are you're in love. Which means there's probably only one thing to do: Throw this book out the window. Because you're no longer obligated to learn another thing about the whys and wherefores of dating. You've now started down a completely different path, a path bound for Significant Otherdom. You are now in an Official Relationship, clues to which can be found in many other books, most of them written by bona fide relationship authorities who actually know what the hell they're talking about.

Still have questions? Worried about what to do if things *don't* work out? Then read on for a few final tidbits.

## DATING ADVICE A-GO-GO

*Once upon a time a young man fell in love with a young woman. So he did everything he could think of to please her and to anticipate her every wish. He was considerate, courteous, and respectful; he never looked at another girl; he was always on tap when she wanted him . . . the young woman was bored stiff. Then she met another young man. This second young man used to get drunk, call her names in front of her friends, and beat the daylights out of her. He took her money, went out with other women, and never telephoned her when he said he would . . . she fell madly in love and ran away with him.*

—HELEN BROWN NORDEN, *THE HUSSY'S HANDBOOK*, 1936

Dating is not a simple business. Even trying to condense its most basic precepts into a two-hundred-page manual is a ridiculous operation—like trying to stuff a hundred pounds of horseshit into a ten-pound bag, as an old boss used to say. What about birth control, you ask? (Use it.) Or developing a crush on your best friend's boyfriend? (Lose it.) Or rebounding? Or cybersex? Or blogs? Why do so many beautiful women treat nice guys like crap? Why do so many nice guys get kidnapped by aliens (what else could explain those mysterious disappearances)? Will

I find my soul mate? Does my butt look big in these jeans? The questions go on and on. For some, there are no answers; for others, a few final insights.

## WHO BRINGS THE CONDOMS AND WHEN?

Everybody brings them, all of the time, according to "Dategirl" columnist Judy McGuire. "People should always be prepared," she says. "Have them in your house and have them in your wallet." However, don't carry the same condoms around in your wallet for years on end (they'll erode), and make sure they're completely tucked out of sight, especially during those first preliminary dates. Nothing's more galling than glancing over at a new date's jeans and seeing the unmistakable outline of a Trojan in their front pants pocket—except perhaps what Jeff, a 25-year-old single from New York, did.

### Hard Pack

*I met up with this girl a few years ago—back when you were able to smoke indoors. We went out for coffee, and I took my box of cigarettes out of my pocket and set them on the table. The girl gave me this really weird look, and I had no clue as to why. Until a few minutes later, when I reached for my cigarettes and discovered it was actually a box of condoms. Apparently, my cigarettes were in the other pocket. As you can imagine, I felt like a complete asshole.*

Some women are leery about stocking condoms at their house ("Guys think it looks bad"). But don't even go there. Instead, think like a Boy Scout—be prepared.

## IS IT KOSHER TO BLOG ABOUT YOUR LOVE LIFE?

No, according to Peter Post of the Emily Post Institute. "What goes on behind the bedroom door ought to stay behind the bedroom door. I'm not sure why people have this need to tell the world about their sexual escapades. It doesn't make a whole lot of sense to me. What's the difference between that and setting up a video camera and filming your escapades and then putting that on the Web, like Paris Hilton? They're both a total invasion of the other person's privacy."

If you *do* decide to throw etiquette to the wind and blog anyway, don't name names (or use identifiable details) unless you're fully prepared for the consequences (payblog is a bitch). And as tempting as it might be to read your lover's blog, try not to, if you can help it. Between poetic license, skewed perspective, and shameless pandering, you may find you don't fare as well as you'd hoped. Or worse—you don't even warrant a mention.

## ARE THERE RULES OF CONDUCT FOR THE FUCK BUDDY?

Yes, says Judy McGuire. "You both have to be equally interested and disinterested. You should never call the person the day after. And you should keep sleepovers to a minimum—it's when you start having breakfast together that attachments start to happen."

McGuire also offers a word of warning: Women are usually more susceptible to "buddy love" than men, due to our basic biological makeup. "We have the traitor within—oxytocin. It's released during orgasm—and also during childbirth. It makes you feel closer to someone and helps you to bond with them." Consider yourself warned.

## WHY WON'T PEOPLE COMMIT?

Because they don't like you enough to commit. Or at least they don't like you enough *at that moment in time.* And, fascinatingly enough, because their brains haven't wired themselves for commitment yet. Along with mapping the brains of infatuated couples, scientists have also mapped those involved in serious relationships. Apparently, scans of couples involved in LTRs showed activity in an area of the brain linked to long-term commitment. What's even more interesting is that scientists at Emory University in Atlanta have been able to isolate an element that turns promiscuous males into committed males by activating this particular area of the brain. So far, the experiments have been conducted only on a ratlike animal known as a vole. If they are ever able to put that formula into pill form (Commitra? Fidelis? Lovium?), my guess is it would outsell Viagra in about three hours.

What often happens, of course, is six months after you break up with your beloved commitment-phobic, you find out they're getting married to somebody else. What's up with that? In a word, timing. A lot of people will say they're not into marriage or commitment, but truth be told, it's just that they're not ready for it *yet.* Whether they're not ready for it with you or not ready for it ever is up for interpretation.

For many people, getting married is all about finding the exact right person—once you meet them you marry, whether you're 26 or 46 or 66 (the age at which Gloria Steinem married for the first time). But others are less discriminating about the person; it's more a matter of finding the right time. They basically date around (some would say play around) until they're tired, and then they just grab whatever looks good and settle down with that. Although this is frustrating for those who invest a lot of time and energy in a relationship without seeing it come

to fruition, that's life. As Peter Post says, "You can't make somebody like you." More importantly, why would you want to?

## WHY DON'T MEN ASK WOMEN OUT ANYMORE?

According to the authors of *He's Just Not That Into You*, the only
reason a man doesn't approach a woman is because he doesn't
want to. "If he likes you, trust me, he will ask you out," they
write. Mason Grigsby, co-author of *Love at Second Sight*, agrees,
to a certain extent. "If a guy doesn't feel there's an attraction, he
won't ask," he says. "That's just human nature. But historically,
men have always had to approach women. And if you talk to men
about how often they get rejected, they'll tell you—it gets wearing after a while."

So wearing that they've simply given up asking? "Maybe men
are afraid of rejection," he says. "They've lost confidence. Their
egos aren't that good. My number-one dating tip for women is to
be proactive about meeting people. If you're in an elevator with a
guy with a nice-looking tie, comment on it. It lets the man know
you're open to a conversation. Most men think women are not
open to conversation, they've been shut down so much. You've got
to let people know that you're open and friendly."

## WHAT IF SOMEONE COMES ON REALLY, REALLY STRONG REALLY, REALLY FAST?

Does it mean they like you? Does it mean they're the one? Only
if you live in 1942, sadly. While most of us have been weaned
on movies that glamorize the strong pursuit, in today's world it
can often mean something completely different—a controlling or
erratic personality.

"It's definitely a red flag," says Ann Rule, author of a dozen
or more books on serial killers and psychopaths. While we all like

it when a date shows interest in us, showing too much interest too soon (i.e., an inordinate amount of flowers, jewelry, drop-ins, phone calls, pressure for commitment, and/or sex) can be trouble—perhaps not psychotic stalker trouble, but definitely something wonky.

"The freaky guys tend to be those romantic 'I love you' guys," says Grigsby. "They're trying to get control over you. Charming, wonderful men can turn out to be con men who just know how to play women to get their money or whatever. If you meet a guy who seems super-perfect—that's the guy you watch out for." In other words, if they seem too good to be true, they probably are. Damn!

## IS IT A BAD THING TO REBOUND?

Obviously, we're all pretty vulnerable after we come out of a long-term relationship, and throwing ourselves into the arms of someone new and wildly different can seem like the best medicine in the world. While many people prefer to recycle an ex during this time (choosing the devil they know, as it were), others decide to pioneer uncharted territory.

Using a new lover as a palette cleanser can work, but it can also be risky. For one thing, not everybody appreciates being treated like a between-course bite of cheese. For another, when we're in the throes of grief, our judgment is not always as sound as it could or should be. Just ask Ken, a 34-year-old single from Philadelphia.

### Creature Feature
*I had just left a relationship of twelve years and was determined to find someone completely different, so I started dating*

*this German woman whose husband had just died (she kept his ashes in an urn in the back of her car, which should have been my first clue). She was new to town and after two dates, I moved in with her at her request. She didn't speak English very well, and at first I thought her "different mannerisms" were due to translation issues. But after a while I realized she had mental problems. One day I came home from work, and everything that I owned was out on the sidewalk. When I asked her why, her answer was "I don't know why I do that." I'd had enough, so I grabbed all of my stuff and left. Then a couple days later, I realized I still had a movie rented in her name in my car, so I drove by her house, saw her outside, and tossed it onto the sidewalk. Two days later, the police came and pulled me from my mother's house (where I was staying), telling me I had violated a restraining order and was wanted for assault . . . Suddenly, I was in jail (I guess it didn't help that the movie was* Cape Fear*).*

## SHOULD I REVEAL MY FEELINGS?

Some argue that letting a new lover know that you care for them is folly. "The most certain way of losing prestige is to let a man see that he occupies a more important place in your mind than you in his," writes Doris Langley Moore in *The Technique of the Love Affair* (1928). "Good or bad, merciful or ruthless, all human creatures are the same in this—the knowledge that there is a soul desperate with devotion before them can only excite pity or amusement, exactly as if they saw the other groveling not in the spirit but in the flesh."

But there's a distinct difference between letting someone know you like them and letting them know you're a doormat.

In an era of flaky ambivalence and relentless ennui, an honest expression of affection can be as refreshing as a Listerine pocket pack. Don't be afraid to let someone know, either through word or deed, that you care.

"On my first official date with this fella, we decided to stay in, cook dinner, and watch a movie," says Kathy, a 32-year-old single from Charleston. "He asked what he could bring, and as a good Southerner, my patent response was 'nothing.' He persisted, however, so I finally responded with a cheeky, 'Well, I could use one of those big bags full of cash.' When he arrived, he handed me this white cotton bag, with a Sharpied dollar sign, filled with change. I discovered later that he had cut up his own bedsheet for the bag. His attention to detail was not lost on me, and we've been dating ever since."

## WHY DO SO MANY GUYS JUST DISAPPEAR?

First of all, they haven't actually disappeared. Nor have they died or been stricken with polio or fallen down that old well on their parents' property (and you were so sure!). They've simply broken up with you and neglected to mention it. Why? Because guys hate confrontation even more than they hate sappy Meg Ryan movies (except that one where she played that crazy chick and looked really hot).

If it makes you feel any better, they've been doing it for ages. "Why didn't I hear from him again?" writes Nina Farewell in *The Unfair Sex*, 1953. "This plaintive cry has echoed in the heart of every woman at some time or other in her life."

And they do it to each other, too. "I have definitely come across my share of flakes," says Jeff, a 36-year-old Seattle single. "Guys for whom even simple dating (even if it's not explicitly exclusive) represents such a loss of freedom and spontaneity that they simply short-circuit themselves into a tizzy and vanish from the face of the earth. I know they're out there somewhere. Probably the same place as my lost socks."

Obviously, all of us want some kind of closure when we break up, even if it hurts. No answer is no answer, right? Unfortunately, with the Amazing Disappear-Os of the world (women have been known to do this as well), no answer is the only answer we're ever going to get. "This type of rejection is a little more difficult to understand and deal with," writes Grigsby, "since everything appears fine and then there is nothing at all."

But truly, what's to understand? Those of us schooled in *Law and Order* (or real law, for that matter) know that silence usually implies consent. So go ahead—ask your questions. Have they broken up with you? Silence. Are they a total coward for not doing it like any decent person would? Silence. Are they going to rot in some special circle of hell dedicated to the weak and the vile? Silence. Do they have a really small dick? Silence. You can amuse yourself like this for hours—or, better yet, you can quit obsessing about these missing mates and find somebody with better manners. Trust me, they're out there.

## AND FINALLY, WHAT'S THE BEST WAY TO GET RID OF A DATE?

Loan them money.

# CHAPTER 8

# BREAKING UP WITH YOUR DATE

*If you wish to get rid of him because he has begun to bore you, or you have found someone else, or you suspect he will never propose—deal with him kindly. After all, he is human, he has shared many pleasant hours with you—and besides, you may want him back some day.*

—Nina Farewell, *The Unfair Sex*, 1953

Who knows how it happened? Maybe he slept with his boss one too many times. Maybe she went to a ghost-hunting convention and was never seen or heard from again. Or maybe your love simply faded like bath towels in the sun. Whatever the case, a breakup is in the wind.

Unless you're 12 or a Trappist monk, you know how unpleasant a trip to the dump can be—for either party. Is there a *good* way to end things with a boyfriend or girlfriend? That's debatable. But there are definitely a few bad ones out there. Cheating, for instance. Or just pretending there's no problem whatsoever until one day you come home and hit your lover over the head with a lamp. Some people bring in a pinch hitter to do the dirty deed: Breakup by Proxy. Others fire off a barrage of accusations and then storm off: the Ammo Dump. But there are a few more.

# DON'T MENTION IT

One of the worst ways to handle a breakup is to simply not mention that it happened. Women, in particular, are familiar with this popular technique, wherein their boyfriends simply vanish without having the decency to mention that the relationship is over. Obviously it's over, otherwise you'd still be nuzzling on the couch and calling each other goofy names. Instead, you're sending text messages into a black hole and spending your valuable time wondering, worrying, wearying.

Is this a decent thing to do? No. Do people do it anyway? You betcha. In fact, the Psychic Breakup (I'm thinking of sleeping with a number of women between one and ten) seems to be growing in popularity. Of course, it's got a ways to go if it wants to compete with the Big Switcheroo, a long-standing breakup technique in which an old partner is slowly eased out of the picture and a new one eased in until suddenly, you realize you've officially become number two.

"I think it's a mistake to date when you're still involved with another person and have neglected to tell them you're no longer interested," says Sonia, 29. "It demonstrates lack of resolve, immaturity, and is just across-the-board disturbing. Which is not to say I haven't done it myself."

As you might imagine, the Big Switcheroo has its kinks. Just ask Robert, a 37-year-old single from Seattle.

### That Niggling Feeling

*I was seeing a woman for a while and ended up spending the night with her one Saturday. And about nine the next morning, we're both lying in bed naked and out the front window I see this brown van pull up. All of a sudden, the woman starts freaking out. "Oh shit! Oh shit!" she says, putting on her bathrobe and her slippers. Then tells me to stay put and goes outside.*

*It's cold out, and she's out there for a while talking all excitedly to this guy in the van. After a while, he speeds off, burning rubber, and she comes back in and tells me that apparently, she'd forgotten to end things with this guy. I'm just relieved he didn't have a key.*

Why is breaking up so hard to do? Throw a rock and you'll find a reason. Because it makes you look like a heel. Because it means having to act like a grown-up. Because inertia (the Viagra of dating for its ability to keep things going long after that loving feeling is gone) is one powerful force. Because *not* breaking up means you can still keep all of your options open and avoid all those nasty confrontations. Because breaking up with someone *hurts*, which explains why so many people will go to such great lengths to avoid it. They'll leave incriminating evidence around their apartments for their partners to find (the Passive-Aggressive Breakup). They'll act like bums and wait for you to do the dumping (the DIY Dump). They'll even use friends to set traps.

"This guy I'd been dating for about four months decided that he wanted to break up with me," says Lisa, 38, of Seattle. "So he asked his best friend to come on to me to see if I would take the bait. The problem was his best friend turned out to be gay and instead of coming on to me, he came out."

## THE DIGITAL DUMP

Of course, many people do manage to dredge up the strength and resolve to actually break up with their dates. The problem is, they do it via email. Or voice mail. Or through some impartial third party such as DumpADate.com, which will send a private prerecorded message (and/or lovely floral bouquet) to the person you don't want to see anymore.

In our ever more responsibility-free world, in fact, breaking up with someone face-to-face is becoming almost passé. The Digital Dump is now so common—and so handy—that Internet dating sites have started incorporating it into their services.

FUN FACT: In a survey of four thousand singles conducted by Match.com, 14 percent said they had broken up with someone via email, 20 percent said someone had broken up with them via email, and 14 percent had had it happen both ways; 53 percent had never been involved in a digital dump.

"Match and Yahoo personals now have canned rejection statements that you can send to people," says Albert, a 69-year-old single from San Francisco. "You only have to click a button and you can send a message that says, 'You're a nice person but I don't think we're a match.' You never even have to contact them. It's hard rejecting people, but I think that's being rather cowardly."

Cowardly or not, it's quick, it's easy, and it's becoming more and more acceptable, at least for those short-term Internet flings. When it comes to LTRs, of course, any kind of Digital Dump is bad juju.

"A friend of mine actually left a message on a woman's answering machine to break up with her," says Robert, a 37-year-old single from Olympia. "He couldn't understand that you should break up with a woman in person. Especially if you've been sleeping with her for over a year."

Still, voice mail and digital breakups do trump an invisible dump. They can even provide a safe platform for clearing up misunderstandings, airing grievances, and expressing feelings that are often difficult to put into words, especially when a vase is careening towards your head at 90 miles an hour.

# THE PERSONAL TOUCH

If people have to choose their poison, though, most prefer the face-to-face breakup. It's considerate, it's respectful, and it's the decent thing to do.

Unfortunately, it's also dangerous. Not only do you have to worry about flying furniture and flailing fists, there's always the chance you'll get hit up alongside the head with an ugly truth. As a result, even those folks who have the decency to go the personal route will try to arrange things in such a way as to avoid the inevitable confrontation—or conflagration.

One common method is the Public Dump, often engineered to occur at a crowded location, such as a restaurant during its busy dinner hour. Even though the Public Dump has been known to backfire ("The chocolate sundae she poured over his head must have been awfully sticky," writes Calvin, a 40-year-old single, about one such incident), some people swear by it.

What do the experts say?

"It's best to break up with someone in person," says Peter Post. "But you don't want to do it in a public place. If you do, you're just compounding their angst and worry. Now they have to think about all those people around them who can see that they're upset."

But what if it's a really, really nice restaurant, the kind often employed in the Wine, Dine, and Dump?

"Trying to bribe somebody into not being mad at you is not going to work," says Post. "The last thing a person cares about while somebody is telling them they don't want to see them again is that they're sitting in a really nice restaurant."

What's the most polite way to break up in person?

**FUN FACT:** In a survey of 10,000 singles conducted by Match.com, 87 percent said they would rather hear the truth (even if it hurt) when someone broke up with them than some sugar-coated lie.

# Best/Worst Ways to Break Up

WHAT'S THE *WORST* WAY TO BREAK UP WITH SOMEONE?

By not actually telling them and simply refusing contact. That or cheating on a person.

—Bethany, 28, Seattle

My ex-boyfriend slept with my neighbor, who claimed to be a lesbian.

—Britt, 30, Seattle

To let the relationship drag on and have no intention of marrying them or pursuing anything long-term, then to call it off after a few years.

—Kate, 26, San Francisco

I was dating this girl, and I took her sister to a wedding. She didn't like that too much and broke into my car that night, peed in it, and left me a note saying she hated me.

—Mark, 23, Seattle

Dumping them on Valentine's Day, the way my last girlfriend did.

—Jon, 50, Bellingham

Any time I have to break up with someone, it's a bad breakup. I never want to hurt their feelings, so I just try to edge my way out slowly. Or just stop calling. I'm horrible at it.

—Jesse, 27, Seattle

When you're backed into a corner, surrounded by her 250-pound buff brothers.

—Calvin, 45, Seattle

## WHAT'S THE *BEST* WAY TO BREAK UP WITH SOMEONE?

Just be honest. It works. No false promises, just the plain truth.

—DESIREE, 48, NORFOLK

Men need to be better at being direct when ending things. Girls like closure. We want to know why. I can handle hearing it. Are you man enough to tell me?

—KARI BETH, 30, SEATTLE

Be honest and up-front. Breakups hurt no matter what, but don't cheat before breaking up. Try to resolve the issues, or break up and then date others. Stop the games!

—DANIEL, 43, MILWAUKEE

I don't think there is a good way. Whatever you say and whatever you do, someone's feelings will be hurt.

—BETHANY, 28, SEATTLE

Tell them that you are not right for each other and you do not want to waste their time in finding the perfect soul mate. Do it quickly and don't let a relationship drag on.

—KATE, 26, SAN FRANCISCO

Just be honest and do it in person. The best method is to be blunt. I have found that no matter how many nice things you say, nobody remembers them. One woman I broke up with was upset that I took her to dinner to break up with her. I just didn't want to do it to her while she had an empty stomach. That's what you get for being nice.

—ROBERT, 37, OLYMPIA

"You have to be honest with the person, but that doesn't mean you need to be nasty," says Post. "Basically, just respect their feelings. If you're going to break up with them, don't do it at your home and then make them have to walk home afterward. Do it someplace private, maybe even at *their* place so you can leave and they can be alone to deal with their upset emotions."

And no matter how you break up with someone, make sure that you make it clear that it *is* the end.

"Men these days are entirely too careful, to the point of leaving loose ends," says Karen, 31, of Chicago. "We women love to hang on to the slightest glimmer of hope. I prefer a man to just be honest—but not rude—and leave no unanswered questions. We're not going to fall apart and die if a guy isn't into us, although it might seem like it at the time. I wish guys would stop treating us like that. Really, get over yourselves."

## FRENEMIES

Is it possible to remain friends with someone after you've broken up? And not just for the usual white-hot breakup sex or occasional bit of recycling that generally goes on after a split? Sometimes yes. "I've been best friends with an old boyfriend for something like seven years," says Jennifer, 24, of New York. Other times no. "The only place I'd like to see my ex is in hell," says Deanna, 40, of San Diego.

Staying friends with an ex can seem impossible during the split, but if both parties have been relatively decent to each other (i.e., kept the cheating, lying, abuse, and burning of treasured mementos to a minimum), it's not inconceivable that a friendship can blossom out of the romantic detritus. Just give yourself some time.

"No matter how civil a breakup starts, it can turn ugly if you try to keep hanging out or try to transition to friendship too soon," warns Clayton, 32. "Love turns to hate and poison before it dies."

Sometimes, though, it's not just a poisonous ex that you have to worry about. Third parties can interfere with the healing process.

"I broke up with this girl that I'd been seeing for a long time, and now her three brothers want to kill me," says Jayme, 32, of San Bernardino. "One of them keeps calling me at two in the morning, leaving messages about how he's going to slice off my fucking balls and feed them to the dogs because I hurt his sister. His sister and I are fine—I haven't even told her what her brothers are doing because she doesn't need to worry about her crazy family. But it's been tough. I can't even go out in public without some friend of theirs coming up and punching me in the face."

Obviously, emotions can run high after a breakup. Some people assuage their anger in the arms of a new lover. Others embrace it by choosing revenge. And then there's Eric, a 27-year-old single from Iowa City, who somehow managed to combine both.

### The Good, the Bad, and the Ugly

*When we broke up, my ex stabbed me, threw me out of my own apartment, then continued to live there while I paid the rent. So I slept with his new boyfriend, and then told him after we had sex-with-the-ex-sex. Later, over martinis, I told him that I'd slept with a lot of men when we were dating (not true-ish), and then I made him apologize and yelled at him. In short, I sort of made him completely crazy until he committed himself for a while. Oops. Other breakups have been better, though. With one fellow, I sat him down, said I didn't want to see him anymore, and as*

*it turned out, he agreed. After that, we became great friends. We*
*still talk and still see each other every once in a while. In fact,*
*we're much better friends than boyfriends.*

Many people cling to the hope that they'll reunite with an ex. They'll beg and plead and refuse to accept facts, even when you show up at some function with a $300 bouquet and eight brides-maids. They'll do anything to get back into your good graces—or your bed, which is usually how the reunion is finally accom-plished. Unfortunately, these relapses have more to do with sex than second thoughts, which can lead to confusion and/or a tire iron up alongside the head when your ex sees you out on the town with your fabulous new love interest. Unless you're a true glut-ton for punishment (or you have a heart of stone), keep sleepovers with the ex to a minimum (and if you do indulge in a few, don't fight, just fornicate).

## MOVING ON

For most of us, though, there's usually only one breakup that completely takes us out at the knees and turns us into a quiv-ering glob of snot—the first one.

"A good friend of mine always tells this story at parties about her first breakup," says Amy, 32, of Santa Fe. "Apparently, it was totally out of the blue, and even though the guy kept trying to be nice about it, throwing out all the standard lines—it's not you, it's me, I'm sorry but I just need to move on, blah blah blah—she just wasn't getting it. In fact, she swears that at one point, she sort of tripped and ended up clutching his leg as he was trying to get away, screaming, 'But whhyyyyy? Whyyyyyyyyyy?' She's never had trouble with breakups after that. I guess once you go through something like that, you learn."

Breakups can hurt even years after the fact (just ask anyone trying to exorcise the Ghost of Relationships Past from their life). And clinging to our dignity (as opposed to someone's leg or some offhand remark—"He said he loved seeing me, *loved* seeing me, so what he's trying to tell me is that he still *loves* me, right?") can be difficult and draining, particularly after months—or years—of really stinky behavior. Sometimes it's easier and more satisfying (at least at the time) to cling to something else, like a mad desire for revenge. Is this smart?

"Overall, revenge is a bad idea," says Anna Jane Grossman, cofounder of BreakupNews.com and coauthor of *It's Not Me, It's You: The Ultimate Book of Breakups*. "But if it has to be done, it should be done with a sense of humor, nothing life threatening or career damaging. One woman posted a story on our site about how she loosened all the seams on a suit that her ex-boyfriend had left at her apartment. When he finally came and got it and tried to put it on, the whole thing just fell apart. It was just a suit, so it wasn't going to make or break him. Breakups are too prevalent and too passing—there's no point in ruining someone's life over one."

Especially when *your* life is what counts.

If you're on the receiving end of a breakup, by all means cry, curse, spit, seduce, and spend as much money as you can afford on shoes, stereo equipment, and sexy lingerie—whatever it takes to get you through the initial shock wave. Bad-mouth the ungrateful wretch to your friends, mock their sexual prowess (or lack thereof), and fill your computer (or public bathroom walls) with reams of embarrassingly bad poetry. But don't be an asshole. Suppress those urges to post ugly naked pictures of your ex on the Internet, to call their mother or boss and reveal some disturbing sexual predilection, to report them to the IRS, ASPCA, Homeland Security. Fantasize about any and all of those things to your heart's content, but don't act. And certainly don't throw in the towel.

Instead, throw your butt in gear. Go on vacation. Buy some new toys. Paint your kitchen. Learn Portuguese. Why? Because the best revenge is living well (writing a best-selling novel or discovering a new erectile dysfunction drug aren't bad options either). Yes, you have anger to deal with—we all do—but instead of using that anger to pulverize your ex's vintage Mustang with a sledgehammer, consider boxing lessons instead. They're safer, they're healthier, and you're far more likely to meet interesting people at the gym than in the county lockup.

Take time for yourself and your wounded heart (or ego, as the case may be) so that the next time you see your ex, you'll be able to get through the ordeal without acting like some revenge-crazed Gorgon. Strive for indifference. And be satisfied if you can get out of there without being physically subdued.

Why? Because it's just good manners.

"Anytime there's a spark between two people and for whatever reason that spark fades, it's very important for both people to still be able to communicate," says Peter Post. "Don't snub them or ignore them; that stinks. I understand how people get into the situation where they just want to do that sort of thing, but they need to be big enough to get by it. You don't need to be romantically involved, but you do need to still be able to talk with them, to simply be polite."

So give up studying *CSI* for clues on undetectable poisons. Quit driving by their house with "your song" blasting on the stereo. Stop obsessing about *them* and instead, start thinking about *yourself.* Throw a huge dinner party to celebrate your new single status. Leaf through the newspaper to see what's shaking in your town. Buy some new dating duds. Get yourself a haircut. And polish up that online profile.

Because, wonder of wonders, my friend, you are back out there.

# CONCLUSION:
# IS DATING NECESSARY?

Seventy-five years ago, a Reno judge by the name of George A. Bartlett decided to write a book about marriage. After presiding over twenty thousand divorces and hearing one imploding love story after another, he felt it time to pose a simple question to the masses: *Is Marriage Necessary?*

Considering the horror stories swapped by today's singles of mannerless morons and bombastic blind dates, one might ask the same question of dating or hooking up or whatever you call that thing we do these days. Is this whole thing necessary? Do we really *have* to go out there?

The simple answer is no.

There's no shame in choosing to remain single—for a month, a year, or even a lifetime. In fact, in recent years there's been a bit of an upsurge in groups advocating the single life, most notably the Quirkyalone movement, whose members "enjoy being single . . . and generally prefer to be alone rather than dating for the sake of being in a couple."

No one is holding a gun to your head, forcing you to spend time with an endless array of dullards and drama queens as you relentlessly search for that "one" magical mate. Sure, between the family pressure, the media preoccupation, and that good old biological imperative, it can *feel* like you're being nudged down some dating gangplank, but truly, the choice is yours. Life is livable—even enjoyable—all on your own.

"Being single is not a death sentence," says Jane Ganahl, singles columnist for the *San Francisco Chronicle*. "For many people, it's a very satisfying lifestyle."

And for others, admittedly, it can get a bit on the lonely side. Our bed grows cold. Our hand needs holding. We yearn to share the banal details of our day with somebody who's on our side— either for the short or the long haul. And that's when our current system of courtship, for better or worse, becomes a necessity.

Is dating a perfect system? Hardly. It would be a miracle if it were; it's only a hundred years old, years that have taken us from the Model T to the space shuttle, from whalebone corsets to the thong, from chaperoned callers to the booty call. For every generation, there's been a different set of rules—some marching forward, others trudging back. For every decade, the dating pool has expanded to include some new bumper crop of singles— teens, tweens, baby boomers, seniors—each with its own ideas and interpretations about how to play the dating and mating game. And just as the development of the automobile and the telephone drastically reshaped the courtship rituals of yesterday, today's new technological wonders—cell phones, email, online dating, cybersex—have left their own indelible mark.

"The challenge that singles have been facing for a long time is not that there are no rules, it's that there are lots of competing systems of rules," says Beth Bailey, historian and author of *From Front Porch to Back Seat: Courtship in Twentieth-Century America* (1988). "In the heyday of dating, there was a clearly voiced set of rules and people knew what they were. But our culture has become less homogenous since the 1950s. There's an enormous amount of cultural variation. So it's confusing."

What can be done to ease this confusion?

"Communication," says Bailey. "My hope for the future is that people will talk a lot more with one another about what makes sense. They'll be forced to explore some of the old assumptions, like the convention that suggests a woman can't possibly be happy without a man or the only way to get a man is to trick him into marrying you."

Seesawing gender roles, shifting views on love, sex, marriage, morality—chances are we'll be tussling with these hot-button issues a hundred years from now, probably from some subterranean singles bar on Mars. Until then, those of us Out There may find it helpful to remember that dating is just the latest incarnation of an ages-old mating ritual, which in the last century or so has taken us from swapping flower bouquets containing secret declarations of love to swapping lab reports containing secret sexual histories. It may not be the best system, it may not be a system that sticks around for much longer ("Dating is a thing of the past," write the authors of *The Hookup Handbook,* "gone the way of dinosaurs and stirrup pants"), but for the time being, it's the one we've got.

Is dating necessary? For those of us hoping to meet someone we genuinely like—and can possibly one day love—the answer is yes. So let's make the most of it, shall we, and try to keep things as pleasant and as compassionate as we can.

Remember, there are no magic beans when it comes to dating—no secret code words or foolproof formulas. The secret to the system lies within each of us—be the bean!—and within the basics of decent behavior your mother taught you, lo, those many years ago. Treat people with consideration, honesty, and respect. Practice good grooming, due diligence, that dazzling smile. Know the score. Cut your losses. Be patient. Believe in yourself. And keep in mind that when it comes to work or play or life or love, good spelling counts for a lot—as does simply showing up.

# ACKNOWLEDGMENTS

A number of individuals, organizations, and online entities acted as research assistants for this book. Heartfelt thanks go to Abebooks.com, Gene Balk, Craigslist.org, GirlPosse.com, Google Alerts, Abigail Grotke (of MissAbigail.com), LavaLife. com, Match.com, the *New York Times*, OnlinePersonalsWatch. com, PerfectMatch.com, Marla Prouty, the Seattle Public Library, Seattle Writergrrls, and Roger Weaver.

I'd also like to express my gratitude to those professionals who contributed their time and considerable expertise to the project, including authors Mason Grigsby, Anna Jane Grossman, Peter Post, Ann Rule, Suzanne Schlosberg, and Em and Lo (of EmandLo. com); dating/singles columnists Jane Ganahl and Judy McGuire; fashion consultants Susan Levitt and Rebecca Luke; health editor Jane Weaver of MSNBC.com; scientists, scholars, and/or psychotherapists Beth Bailey, Stephanie Coontz, Bella DePaulo, David Givens, Roy Lubit, Jodi O'Brien, Pepper Schwartz, and Tina Tessina, and dating professionals Patti Feinstein, Samantha MacIntosh, Noel McLane, Katherin Scott, Christine Stelmack, Julie Thompson, Elizabeth Tyner, and David Wygant. Thank you all for your generous help and wonderful insights.

Special thanks also to Anne Hurley and the *Seattle Times*, Elizabeth Wales and the Wales Literary Agency, and my colleagues at Book-It Repertory Theatre. A big high five to the crackerjack team at Sasquatch Books who helped produce this labor of love— Terence Maikels, Heidi Schuessler, Julie Van Pelt, Stewart Williams, Sherri Schultz, Bob Suh, Gina Johnston, and Courtney

Payne—singles all. I'd also like to thank the following dear friends for their invaluable assistance: Jeff Card, Judith Chandler, Chris Galvin, Michelle Goodman, Chris Jarvis, Leslie Kelly, Leita McIntosh-Koontz, Heather McKinnon, Laura McLeod, Renate Raymond, and Jarratt Spady.

Finally, I'd like to thank my four sisters—Gloria, Mary, Frances, and Peggy—for all they've given me over the years, and to extend my deep appreciation to the hundreds of singles who graciously shared their most private, poignant and pee-your-pants funny tales from the dating trenches. I could not have done any of this without you.

# AUTHOR PROFILE

NAME: Diane Mapes

GENDER: Female

STATUS: Single

LOCATION: Seattle, Washington

SEEKING: Readers

HAIR/EYES: Blonde / Blue

HEIGHT: 5'4"

BAWDY TYPE: Much to the chagrin of my family, yes

EDUCATION: Bachelor's degree in English/creative writing

OCCUPATION: Freelance writer of articles on dating, the single life, pop culture, travel, television, and more in *Bust*, *Health*, the *Los Angeles Times*, *Mental Floss*, *Seattle Magazine*, the *Seattle Times*, and the recent anthology *Single Woman of a Certain Age*

Erik Stuhaug

DRINKS: One's my limit (I absolutely cannot start any earlier than that)

SMOKES: Only when I'm typing really fast

A LITTLE ABOUT ME: I'm incredibly curious and love to research and write about all kinds of crazy topics—cemeteries, spelunking, naked sushi, and of course, today's singles scene. For the past two years, I've written about dating almost exclusively and have corresponded with hundreds of singles from across the country and as far away as Afghanistan and Australia. When not writing, I like to hang out in used bookstores, trolling for new additions to my ever-growing collection of vintage sex and dating manuals. Other favorite pastimes: antique shopping with my sisters, watching old movies, and playing the accordion (and I wonder why I'm still single).